Receiving fuel from a KC-10A Extender, this F-15C from the 1st TFW, flies a CAP mission configured two external fuel tanks, four AIM-9 Sidewinders and four AIM-7 Sparrow air-to-air missiles. (DOD)

BIRDS OF PREY

Aircraft, Nose Art & Mission Markings of Operation Desert Shield/ Desert Storm

David F. Brown

Schiffer Military/Aviation History
Atglen, PA

Acknowledgements

I am sincerely indebted to my colleagues and nearly one hundred others from around the world who gave of their valuable time to assist me in this endeavor. Their eagerness to help and the abundance of information and images furnished to me have been simply overwhelming. Without these contributions this project would not have reached fruition.

Special thanks are in order for Rena Aikins, Chris Aleong, Michael M. Anselmo, Bob Archer, Sergio Bottaro, Marc Brouyere, Mel Brown, Tony Cassanova, Dick Cole, Robert F. Dorr, Norb Feist, Kevin Foy, John Grech, Mike Grove, Phillip Huston, Randy Jolly/Aero Graphics, Tom Kaminski, Alex Knoops, Michael P. Kopack Sr., Michael P. Kopack Jr., Robert L. Lawson, R.A. London, Terry M. Love, Jeff Rankin-Lowe/Sirius, Charles E. Mesker, J.E. Michaels/ JEM Slides, R.J. Mills Jr., Mark Morgan, Rick Morgan, Paul Osborne, Dave Parsons, Brian Pickering/MAP, Jeff Puzzullo, David Reade, Mike Reyno, Charles T. Robbins, Brian C. Rogers, Philippe Roman, Barry E. Roop, R.E. Rys, Brian Scott, Bob Shane, Robbie Shaw, Keith Snyder, Dennis Smith, Don Spering/AIR, Peter Steinemann, Keith Svendsen, Andy Thomson, Jim Tunney, Scott Van Aken, Achille Vigna, Thomas Walsh, Bryan H. Wilburn, Peter Wilson, Roberto Zambon and Joe Zerbe.

Some of the images appearing on the following pages could not have been obtained were it not for the dedication of certain individuals in various Public Affairs Offices. Therefore I wish to extend a special thank you to Jay Barber, Seymour Johnson AFB; Bert Byers, NAS Cecil Field; Bobbie Carlton, CPO, USN; Lester Caroll, Capt., SCANG; Russell D. Egnor, USN News Photo Division; ACE Ewers, NAS Oceana; J.C. Frier, Air Operations, NAS Oceana; Liz Grandin, A1C, USAF; Sandra A. Henry, Elgin AFB; David M. Kamiya, British Aerospace; Arnold Kozloski, Capt. USMC; Velda McCoy, LCpl., USMC; Cara Rey, Capt., USAF; Troy Snead, NAS Norfolk; Steven M. Titunik, LTC, USA; Janet Tucker, Maj., USAF; James F. Tynan, Capt., USAF; Carol Watson, Lt., USN; and to those whom I have somehow overlooked.

Finally, to the following who gave generously of their time, providing me with a wealth of information concerning the air war in the Gulf, I extend a 'well done' and thank you: Brian Allen, Capt., USAF; Ted Beaton, Capt., USAF; Bruce Bole, LCdr., USN; Jim Carnahan, Maj., USAF; Brian Conlon, Capt., USAF; Chris Dinenna, Capt., USAF; William L. Gall, MSgt., PAANG; Merrill R. Karp, Col., USAF; John Leenhouts, Cdr., USN; Rich Linnekin, Capt., USMC; Steve McPerson, Capt., USAF; Larry Muench, LtCol., USAF; Steven Mugg, LtCol., USMC; Stephen Otto, Lt., USAF; Stephan Pomeroy, Maj., USMC; J.P. Reilly, Capt., SCANG; Pat Rink, Capt., USMC; Don Searles, Col., USAF; Harmon Stockwell, Maj., USMC; Steven Tate, Capt., USAF; Craig Underhill, Capt., USAF, Frank Urben LtCol., USAF; Chip Utterback, LtCol., USAF; Joe Walsh, Capt., USAF; and George Walton, LtCol., USAF.

Last, but not least, I thank my sweetheart and wife Christina, who somehow manages to put up with my passion to photograph and write about airplanes, even when it borders on eccentricity.

Authors Note

As the 100 hour ground war in the Gulf came to a conclusion, I commenced the lengthy process of arranging to visit as many Desert Storm flying units as possible. Following the submission of literally mountains of paperwork, and after making numerous appointments with the proper base and squadron personnel I began to visit bases documenting the aircraft, nose art and mission markings from the Gulf war. I made my first stop at Langley AFB., 8 March 1991. It seemed appropriate that the first fighter unit to deploy to the Gulf, the 1st TFW, should also be the first to rotate home.

During the following eight months I criss-crossed the continental United States documenting the aircraft, nose art and mission markings from the air campaign. One week I was in northern Maine photographing B-52s at Loring AFB., a week later I was in Florida photographing A-7Es, F/A-18s and S-3s at NAS Cecil Field. On one ten day trip I managed to put 2800 miles on a rental car tracking down Desert Storm aircraft based in the southwest.

By July, 1991 I realized I was in a race against time. The special markings, the nose art and even the aircraft were disappearing. The later caused by a reduction in force and subsequent down-sizing of the US armed forces. As for aircraft markings, specifically those applied to TAC aircraft, it was obvious that they were being expunged. In military parlance, the aircraft had to be 'sanitized' in order to conform to current regulations dictating aircraft appearance. Oddly enough, as TAC went about removing special markings, SAC, which oversaw the operations of the Gulf War tanker and bomber fleet was encouraging the reapplication of nose art removed for fear of offending our Saudi hosts.

By October 1991, after having flown and driven several thousand miles, I came to the conclusion that I alone would not be able to document fully the aircraft that participated in the Gulf war. It was time to put down the cameras and solicit the assistance of my colleagues, and activate my word processor. My decision was in no small part due to my wife's revelation that our two year old was calling the UPS delivery man 'Daddy.' I had been away from home too long!

From a pragmatic viewpoint it became apparent that to document accurately every aircraft type, all of the nose art and mission markings was beyond the realm of possibility. These markings not only varied from deployment to home coming, they varied from sortie to sortie. I believe what I have managed to assemble on these pages represents the largest collection of Desert Shield/Desert Storm aircraft, nose art and mission markings recorded to date. I sincerely hope you will find it interesting and historically rich in information relevant to the art, markings and paint schemes applied to the myriad of aircraft that participated in the Gulf war.

David F. Brown
Spring Grove, PA

On the cover
Front:
Within 38 hours of receiving notification of their deployment to Saudi Arabia, F-15C's of the 71st TFS, were standing alert and flying Combat Air Patrol from Dhahran, Saudi Arabia. (DOD)

Rear:
Assigned to the SEAD (Suppression of Enemy Air Defenses) mission, F-4G Wild Weasels like this example for the 561st TFS/35th TFW, were among the most active aircraft taking part in combat operations during Desert Storm. (Don Spering/AIR)

Book Design by Robert Biondi
Technical editing by R.J. Mills, Jr., and J.E. Michaels

First Edition

Library of Congress Catalog Number: 92-62609

Printed in the United States of America.
ISBN: 0-88740-472-3
We are interested in hearing from authors with book ideas on related topics.

Published by Schiffer Publishing Ltd.
77 Lower Valley Road
Atglen, PA 19310
Please write for a free catalog.
This book may be purchased from the publisher.
Please include $2.95 postage.
Try your bookstore first.

DEDICATION

They endured ungodly weather conditions, diseases they had never heard of, cultural clashes, and a complete lack of alcoholic beverages. After working many sixteen and eighteen hour days, they returned to sleeping quarters that were filled with jet noise and fumes. Through it all they achieved aircraft availability rates far exceeding the peacetime norm. To the men and women who maintained, armed, and flew the aircraft of Operation Desert Shield/Desert Storm, I dedicate this book – for a job well done.

CONTENTS

F-15C, 85-0114, tucks in close to a KC-10A while receiving fuel. A single Iraqi flag below the windscreen represents a MiG-29 'maneuvered into the ground' by Capt. Cesar A. Rodriquez on 19 January 1991. (DOD)

UNITED STATES AIR FORCE, RESERVES AND AIR NATIONAL GUARD

As this publication goes to press there is still much debate concerning which branch of the armed forces reached the Gulf theater of operations first. Some claim it was the transport aircraft of the Military Airlift Command, while others contend that F-15 Eagles of the Tactical Air Command were the first to arrive. Adherents of US Naval aviation point out that two carrier battle groups built around the USS Independence and USS Eisenhower, were the first real deterrent to Saddam Hussein. Even the P-3 Orion community makes a strong argument since P-3Cs of VP-1 were flying combat patrols from Al Masirah AB., Oman, within forty-eight hours of the invasion of Kuwait.

Currently, it has been acknowledged that lead elements of the 1st TFW represented the first US combat unit to establish a base of operations in defense of Saudi Arabia. They arrived in-theater on 8 August, 1990 following a grueling fifteen hour, 8000 mile non-stop flight from Langley AFB., Virginia. Within thirty-eight hours of being notified of the deployment, F-15C's of the 71st TFS, 1st TFW, were standing alert at Dhahran Intl. Apt., Saudi Arabia. This force was joined by elements of the 82nd Airborne Division and five additional fighter squadrons. By the end of August, F-15E Strike Eagles, F-16C/D Falcons, F-4G Wild Weasels, RF-4C Phantom IIs, F-117A Nighthawks, A-10A Warthogs and various reconnaissance aircraft had arrived to form a potent deterrent force.

By January 1991, following phase two of the deployment, approximately 46% of the combat squadrons of the USAF based in the United States were deployed to the Gulf Region. This figure included Air National Guard units from McEntire ANGB, SC., Hancock Field, Syracuse, NY., May Field Reno, NV., and Birmingham AL., and an AFres fighter unit from NAS New Orleans, La. A deployment of such magnitude required a great deal of airlift and aerial refueling. The majority of the fighter units which deployed from the US required no fewer than seven in-flight refuelings. From the standpoint of cargo airlifted, the first six weeks of Desert Shield involved the movement of more tonnage than the entire Berlin Airlift. At center stage was the C-141B Starlifter and C-5 Galaxy with 85% of the combined fleet dedicated to the deployment. The movement of troops and material once reaching the operating theater became the responsibility of the venerable C-130 Hercules. At least 200 Hercules transports were directly assigned to Desert Shield/Desert Storm, and these delivered 300,000 tons of cargo and airlifted 209,000 troops during 47,000 sorties. During the 100 hour ground war, the Hercules flew more than 500 sorties daily.

Among those in the tanker community, it is often repeated that "you can't kick ass without tanker gas." This statement was never truer than during Desert Shield/Desert Storm. During the former, SAC KC-135s and KC-10s delivered 68.2 million gallons of fuel to 14,588 aircraft. Before the cessation of hostilities, this figure had risen to 194 million gallons. A portion of the tanker fleet consisted of ANG and AFres units. On the opening night of the air campaign, 160 tankers were aloft to support the first air strikes by coalition forces. The critical role played by the tankers was significant during the first nights success and remained so throughout the war.

Once established in the Gulf, USAF and ANG units were consolidated into Provisional Wings within Provisional Air Divisions. For example, the 16th Air Division consisted of MAC squadrons operating the C-130E/H Hercules. The 17th Air Division was comprised of SAC and TAC assets. The largest and most diverse Provisional Wing was the 7440th based north of Iraq at Incirlik AB., Turkey. Aircraft assigned to the 7440th consisted of F-15C/D's, F-16C/D's, F-4E/G's, RF-4C's, EF-111's, EC-130's, E-3B's and KC-135's. A special operations detachment from the 39th SOW was also attached to the 7440th but was based at Batman AB., Turkey. The 7440th did not enter the air campaign until its second day because Turkish officials could not reach a decision about launching air strikes from their soil.

On 17 January, at 0220 hours Baghdad time, just as the first of fifty-two Tomahawk cruise missiles were bearing down on targets in Iraq, Task Force Normandy was racing low across the desert approaching the Iraqi border. Composed of Army AH-64 Apache helicopters guided by two Special Operations MH 53J Pave Low III helicopters, Task Force Normandy was about to fire the first shots in the war to Liberate Kuwait. Its mission was to destroy Iraqi early warning radars, thus allowing a sizable strike package to enter Iraq undetected. The task force accomplished its mission with near surgical precision and by 0238 hours the first F-15E Strike Eagles, escorted by F-4G's and EF-111A's, were passing over the burning remnants of the radar sites. In the United States it was 6:45 EST, 16 January, news reports throughout the country were interrupting television broadcasts with reports of furious anti-aircraft fire over Baghdad.

After launching from their base at Khamis Mushait, F-117 Nighthawks of the 415th TFS, flew the length of Saudi Arabia entering Iraqi airspace undetected. Individually they headed to strategic targets in and around Baghdad. As the opening stages of the air war were unfolding, its architect, Lieutenant General Charles A. Horner, was listening to a live CNN broadcast originating from Baghdad. At precisely H hour the broadcast ceased. An F-117 had just delivered a GBU-27, 2000-lb., smart bomb into Baghdad's telecommunication building, the "AT&T building", as it was often referred to. Shortly thereafter the headquarters for the Iraqi Air Force received the same treatment. On this first night of the air campaign, F-117s attacked 31% of the strategic targets in and around Baghdad. During the course of the war, F-117s delivered ordnance on 40% of the strategic targets while flying only 2% of the total combat sorties.

As the F-117's pounded targets in Baghdad, other not-so-stealthy nor state-of-the-art aircraft from another era were attacking surface-to-air missiles sites, industrial complexes, fuel depots and airfields. F-4G Wild Weasels, with combat time acquired in Vietnam, as F-4Es were actively searching for and destroying SAM sites. In the meantime, B-52s, BUFFs as they are affectionately known, were nearly halfway through a historic thirty-five hour combat mission which begun hours earlier at Barksdale AFB., Louisiana. As F-117s struck targets in Baghdad, B-52Gs from the 2nd BW, were preparing to launch conventionally armed AGM-86C cruise missiles. More than seventy B-52Gs participated in the conflict dropping or launching 27,000 tons of ordnance.

Yet another holdover from the Vietnam era, the F-111, emerged from the Gulf war as a swing-wing jack-of-all-trades, a real workhorse. The seventy or so EF/F-111s flew more than 4,000 sorties against bridges, aircraft shelters, nuclear facilities, bunkers and armored vehicles. Against the latter, the F-111 proved quite effective defeating armor, and by wars end was credited with more than 900 tank kills. In the electronic counter measures arena, the EF-111A, Raven or Sparkvark, flew 900 combat sorties clearing a path for USAF and USN strikes by flooding enemy radars with electrons, thereby cloaking the attack force.

The RF-4Cs which deployed in support of Desert Shield/Desert Storm were a little long in the tooth, each having flown for at least twenty-five years. Gulf war RF-4Cs were drawn from the USAF and ANG. The 106th TRS/117th TRW, Alabama ANG, represented the first RF-4C unit to arrive in the Gulf. This squadron consisted of volunteers who were in much demand for their expertise in operating the LOROP equipped version of the RF-4C. LOROP stands for LOng Range Oblique Photography system, which permitted the RF-4C's of the 117th to look deep into Iraq. Although the 117th was relieved by the 192nd TRS/152nd TRW, Nevada ANG, their LOROP modified Phantoms remained in the Gulf. In January 1991, the RF-4C force was bolstered with the arrival of elements from the 12th TRS/67th TRW based at Bergstrom AFB, Texas. Additional RF-4C's arrived from the 38th TRS/26th TRW. This unit deployed to Incirlik AB., Turkey to form the reconnaissance assets of the 7440th Provisional Wing. Throughout Desert Shield/Desert Storm, RF-4Cs flew daylight missions and were used extensively to gather information concerning mobile Scud launchers.

Although no ace emerged from the Gulf war, it would be a reasonable assumption that he would have been a member of an F-15C squadron. A score of thirty-one air-to-air kills were registered by F-15C pilots, giving them the distinction of downing more Iraqi aircraft than the total effort of coalition pilots flying other types of aircraft. This figure includes a MiG-29 Fulcrum and Mirage F.1 which were literally maneuvered into the ground by F-15C pilots.

As the F-15C was clearing the skies, F-15E Strike Eagles were involved in attacking aircraft on the ground and clearing Scuds and their launchers from the northwest corner of Iraq. By using to full advantage the few LANTIRN pods available in conjunction with targeting information provided by the E-8 J-STARS, Strike Eagles were able to significantly reduce the threat of Scud attacks.

With 249 F-16s deployed to the Gulf region, this type was the most numerous combat aircraft to take part in Desert Shield/Desert Storm. A total of 13,500 sorties were flown by a number of F-16 squadrons drawn from units in the US and Europe. During phase two of the Desert Shield build up two ANG F-16A units were sent to the Gulf to supplement USAF F-16 units deployed earlier in the build up. F-16 sorties consisted of Suppression of Enemy Air Defenses (SEAD), FastFAC (Forward Air Control) and Battlefield Area Interdiction (BAI). The 174th TFW, New York ANG, introduced the CAS or Close Air Support version of the F-16 Falcon to combat during the Gulf war. The 174th presently, is the only F-16 unit dedicated to the CAS mission and its Falcons are the only F-16s equipped with the GPU-5, 30mm gun pod.

The A-10 Thunderbolt II, an aircraft the USAF never fully embraced, was dispatched to the Gulf region in numbers exceeded only by the F-16. Although designed as a tank buster, the Warthog, as it is popularly known, flew a variety of missions including hunting Scuds, their launchers and staging areas, attacking airfields, suppressing SAM sites, performing RESCAP, battle field aerial interdiction, and close air support. Coming into its own during the 100 hour war, the A-10A proved its worth by flying close air support missions and destroying hundreds of Iraqi armored vehicles. Although the Iraqi air defense threat forced the A-10 to fly above 10,000 feet, it nevertheless was able to utilize its GAU-8 30mm cannon to good effect against Iraqi armor. The A-10 emerged from the conflict having flown one third of the USAF sorties and accounted for more than half of the Iraqi equipment destroyed.

The 4th TFW(Provisional) was comprised of three F-15 Eagle squadrons, the 335th, 336th and 53rd. In addition, the wing included two F-16A squadrons, the 138th and 157th drawn from the New York and South Carolina Air National Guard. (DOD)

MCDONNELL DOUGLAS F-15 EAGLE

This simple green star on the nose of F-15C, 83-0017, denotes an aerial victory scored against an Iraqi Mirage F.1EQ, during the first hours of the air campaign. The pilot, Capt., Steven Tate, of the 71st TFS, was initially heralded as having shot down the first Iraqi aircraft of the war. Subsequent review of AWACS data and debriefs of other fighter pilots, resulted in Capt. Tate receiving credit for the third aerial victory of the war. (Author)

The first operational F-15 Eagle was delivered to the 58th TFTW at Luke AFB, on 14 November 1974. The 1st TFW, Langley AFB., holds the distinction of being the first operational F-15 Wing. The Eagle has since equipped a total of ten USAF wings, five ANG units and is operated by the Air Forces of three foreign nations, Israel, Saudi Arabia and Japan. Prior to its deployment to the Gulf, the F-15 was known as a fighter pilot's fighter. It emerged from the Gulf as the premier air superiority fighter in the world. During the air campaign, F-15 Eagles accounted for every USAF aerial victory against fixed wing aircraft. The F-15C's from four fighter wings literally cleared the skies of Iraqi aircraft using AIM-7 Sparrow, and AIM-9 Sidewinders air-to-air missles to down more than twenty Iraqi aircraft.

The F-15E Strike Eagle, was instrumental in leading night attacks against mobile Scud launchers. Equipped with LANTIRN (Low Altitude Navigation and Targeting Infra-Red for Night) pods, and its APG-70 radar, the Strike Eagle was able to pinpoint targets under some of the most adverse weather conditions experienced in the region in nearly 100 years. Although armed with AIM-9 Sidewinders, the Strike Eagle remained outside the arena of aerial combat with one notable exception. One enterprising Strike Eagle crew destroyed a hovering Iraqi helicopter with a GBU-10 2000-lb., precision guided bomb.

The 1st TFW was based at one of the newest facilities at Dhahran Intl. Apt. Of interest are the revetments protecting the taxiway from the hardened shelters. (Robert F. Dorr)

F-15C EAGLE AERIAL VICTORIES

DATE	UNIT	SERIAL	CREW	TYPE	WEAPON
JAN.17	58th TFS	85-0125	Capt. Kelk	MiG-29	AIM-7
	58th TFS	85-0105	Capt. Graeter	2XMirage F1	AIM-7
	71st TFS	83-0017	Capt. Tate	Mirage F1	AIM-7
	58th TFS	85-0107	Capt. McGill[1]	MiG-29	AIM-7
	58th TFS	85-0108	Capt. Draeger[2]	MiG-29	AIM-7
19	58th TFS	85-0099	Capt. Pitts	MiG-25	AIM-7
	58th TFS	85-0101	Capt. Tollini	MiG-25	AIM-7
	58th TFS	85-0122	Capt. Underhill	MiG-29	AIM-7
	58th TFS	85-0114	Capt. Rodriquez	MiG-29	ACM
	525th TFS	79-0021	Lt. Sveden	Mirage F1	AIM-7
	525th TFS	79-0069	Capt. Prather	Mirage F1	AIM-7
26	58th TFS	85-0104	Capt. Schiavi	MiG-23	AIM-7
	58th TFS	85-0119	Capt. Draeger	MiG-23	AIM-7
	58th TFS	85-0114	Capt. Rodriquez	MiG-23	AIM-7
27	53rd TFS	84-0025	Capt. Denney	2XMiG-23	AIM-9
	53rd TFS	84-0027	Capt. Powell	MiG-23	AIM-7
				Mirage F1	AIM-7
28	32nd TFS	79-0022	Capt. Watrous	MiG-23	AIM-7
29	58th TFS	85-0102	Capt. Rose[3]	MiG-23	AIM-7
FEB. 2	525th TFS	79-0074	Capt. Masters	IL-76	AIM-7
6	53rd TFS	79-0078	Capt. Dietz	2XMiG-21	AIM-9
	53rd TFS	84-0019	Lt. Hehemann	2XSU-25	AIM-9

DATE	UNIT	SERIAL	CREW	TYPE	WEAPON
7	58th TFS	85-0102	Capt. Murphy	2XSU-22	AIM-7
	58th TFS	85-0124	Col. Parsons	SU-22	AIM-7
	525th TFS	80-0003	Maj. May[4]	Helo	AIM-7
11	525th TFS	79-0048	Capt. Dingee	Helo	AIM-7
	525th TFS	80-0012	Capt. McKenzie	Helo	AIM-7
14	335th TFS	89-0487	Capt. Bennett[5] Capt. Bakke (WSO)	Helo	GBU-10
MAR. 20	53rd TFS	84-0014	Capt. Doneski	SU-22	AIM-9
22	53rd TFS	84-0010	Capt. Dietz	SU-22	AIM-9
	53rd TFS	84-0015	Lt. Hehemann	PC-9	Ejected

ROYAL SAUDI AIR FORCE

DATE	UNIT	SERIAL	CREW	TYPE	WEAPON
JAN.24	13 Sqn.	80-0068	Capt. Al-Shamrani RSAF # 509	2 Mirage F1	AIM-9P

Notes:
1. Capt. McGill was on exchange duty from the USMC
2. Capt. Draeger was from the 59th TFS which did not deploy.
3. Capt. Rose was from the 60th TFS which did not deploy.
4. Maj. May assigned to 22nd TFS, which did not deploy.
5. F-15 Strike Eagle and crew.

MALONEY'S PONY, F-15C, 82-0023, of the 27th TFS, 1st TFW, represented the only F-15 to carry nose art during the Gulf war. This particular F-15C has worn this nose art for several years as a tribute to Lt. Tom Maloney, a P-38 Lightning ace who served with the 27th TFS during World War II. (Close up - Author) (Sideview - DOD)

The yellow fin flash on this 1st TFW F-15C indicates it is assigned to the 27th TFS. Ordnance consists of the standard CAP configuration. (SGT David McLeod)

F-15E strike packages involved as many as twenty-two aircraft including EF-111A's and F-4G's for suppressing enemy air defenses. The Strike Eagles struck targets in two-ship formations 20 to 30 seconds apart. (Author)

Within minutes of the commencement of the air war, waves of Strike Eagles from the 4th TFW(P) struck fixed Scud launchers in northwest Iraq. (Author)

A technique known as 'fly-up attack' was developed in the Gulf to attack fixed Scud sites. Strike Eagles would ingress at 300 feet. Upon reaching their target they would "zoom up" to 20,000 feet, make a 20 degree dive and release their ordnance. Besides precision guided munitions, the F-15E used a combination of MK-82 500-lb and Rockeye cluster bombs. (Author)

'Gulf Spirit', F-15C, 85-0102, was painted prior to the units deployment to the Gulf. This Eagle and a handful of other 33rd TFW F-15Cs received special tail markings for an upcoming "William Tell" exercise. A close up of the markings reveal that it took part in three aerial victories, none of which were scored while flown by Wing Commander Col. Rick Parsons, whose name is inscribed on the side of this F-15C. Although the AMRAAM Advanced Medium-Range Air-to-Air Missile, was carried aboard some F-15Cs deployed to the Gulf, the weapon of choice in the majority of aerial victories was the AIM-7 Sparrow. (Author)

Another view of 85-0114, from the 58th TFS/33rd TFW, following Capt. Rodriquez's second aerial victory scored against a MiG-23 on 26 January. A total of five pilots of the 58th TFS scored at least two aerial victories during and shortly after the Gulf war. (Author) Below: Close up of aerial victory markings on Capt. Rodriquez's F-15C. The green star represents victories by the pilot. The Iraqi flag signifies each victory by that particular F-15. Barely discernible beneath a layer of paint is a much larger star, possibly the first version of kill markings applied immediately after combat. For whatever reason, these larger markings were not adopted. (Author)

Departing for the Gulf on 29 December 1990, the 335th TFS/4th TFW, only possessed ten LANTIRN targeting pods. Strike Eagles used 'buddy lasing' with one F-15E illuminating a target for his wingman. (Author)

The 'BT' tailcode and yellow fin cap distinguish this F-15C as belonging to the 53rd TFS/36th TFW. On 27 January 1991, F-15C, 84-0027 scored two aerial victories downing a MiG-29 and a Mirage F.1. (DOD)

Below: The Strike Eagle carries a crew of two. The pilot flies and navigates while the Weapons System Officer (WSO) identifies targets and releases ordnance. The WSO has a variety of targeting aids including the Hughes AN/APG-70 Synthetic Aperture Radar, Forward Looking Infra-Red and LANTIRN targeting pods. (Author)

Above right: This AN/AAQ-13 pod is always carried on the F-15Es starboard side. The pod is optimized for Forward Looking Infra-red (FLIR) imagery. (Author)

Right: Neat rows of bomb markings cover part of the nose on this 335th TFS Strike Eagle. They attest to the contribution made by Strike Eagles, pilots, WSOs and maintenance personnel during the air campaign. (Author)

An Iraqi pilot at the controls of a PC-9 light attack trainer opted to eject when he observed an F-15C at his 'six o'clock' position. The Eagle, 84-0015, was piloted by Lt. Robert W. Hehemann, of the 53rd TFS and the engagement took place 22 March 1991, nearly a month after the cessation of hostilities. The PC-9 was attacked along with an Iraqi SU-22 after their pilots violated the UN ban on flights by Iraqi fixed wing aircraft. (DOD)

Left: The 174th TFW recently exchanged their A-10A Thunderbolt II's for some of the oldest F-16A's in the inventory. The majority of their Falcons came from the 474th TFW when that unit disbanded. (The unit has since transitioned to the F-16C/D.) (Author)

Below: A pilot of the 138th TFS/174th TFW, goes through final checks prior to departing from Hancock Field, Syracuse New York. "The Boys From Syracuse", represented one of two ANG F-16 units deployed to the Gulf during phase two of the Desert Shield buildup; undoubtedly selected for their expertise in Close Air Support and ability to deploy the GPU-5A Pave/Claw cannon pod. (Author)

MiG-29 and Mirage kill markings on F-15C, 84-0027 of the 53rd TFS/36th TFW. (Marc Brouyere)

Right: Crude but impressive scoreboard on the nose gear door of 138th TFS, F-16A, 79-0399. (Author)

Since their base at Al Kharji, Saudi Arabia was referred to as "Camel Lot", it seemed only appropriate to make reference to it somewhere on a 138th TFS, F-16A. This diminutive cartoon appeared on the nose gear door of an unidentified F-16A of the 138th TFS. (Paul Osborne)

Rather unusual headgear worn by a returning pilot of the 138th TFS. (Paul Osborne)

Right: The 157th TFS/169th TFG, South Carolina Air National Guard comprised the only other F-16 ANG unit to deploy to the Gulf. This example was photographed just hours prior to deploying on a 13 1/2 hour flight to Southwest Asia. It crossed the Atlantic with elements from the 138th TFS, NY ANG. (Tony Cassanova)

Below: The 160th TFS, Alabama ANG, did not deploy to the Gulf. However, this example did, as a replacement aircraft flown alongside the 138th TFS in case one of its Falcons were forced to abort during the 13 1/2 hour flight to Saudi Arabia. (Tony Cassanova)

Above and left: Mission markings were placed in a number of locations on 157th TFS Falcons. Here, two examples display them above the intake and along the canopy rails. (Author)

FAIRCHILD/REPUBLIC A-10A THUNDERBOLT II

The A-10A is officially known as the Thunderbolt II, however, military aircraft are seldom referred to by their official names. In US Air Force service the A-10A, is known to its crew as the 'Warthog' or 'Hog.' The name has more to do with the wart-like rivets covering the A-10A than its appearance. Although nearly orphaned by the USAF, and increasingly relegated to service with the ANG and AFRES, the A-10A was nevertheless deployed to the Gulf in numbers exceeded only by the F-16. During the air campaign the 'Warthog' gained star status proving itself time and again by destroying half the Iraqi equipment accounted for by the USAF.

Its success during the Gulf war surprised everyone except those who flew it. It successfully performed every mission assigned to it. Aside from its built-in tank busting ability, the A-10 was quite adept at attacking Scud launchers, missile sites and airfields. It also participated in at least one RESCAP operation preventing Iraqi troops from reaching a downed Navy pilot. The 'Warthog' even scored two aerial victories against Iraqi helicopters. Five A-10s were destroyed for a loss rate of .062 percent, twenty returned with serious damage, and an additional forty-five 'Warthogs' suffered light damage. Nearly all returning Gulf A-10s displayed art work. Unfortunately, within weeks of returning stateside, this nose art was removed per orders from headquarters TAC.

Left: It is quite evident by the 74 TFS on the vertical stabilizer that this A-10A is assigned to that unit as the squadron commander's aircraft. Of interest is the Sharksmouth. These markings date back to World War II, when the unit was designated the 23rd Fighter Group, the "Flying Tigers." (Kevin Foy)

Below: A red fin cap indicates that this A-10A, is assigned to the 75th TFS/23rd TFW. The 74th and 75th TFSs deployed to the Gulf during Desert Shield. These units were reinforced by pilots and aircraft supplied by the 76th TFS also from the 23rd TFW. (Jim Tunney)

Above and right: Like its namesake, the P-47 Thunderbolt, the A-10 proved it could also absorb a tremendous amount of punishment and bring its pilot home. This example was assigned to the 23rd TFW(P) based at King Fahd International Airport, Saudi Arabia. (DOD)

The business end of the A-10A, its GAU-8A Avenger cannon which is capable of firing rounds at a rate of 2000 per minute. During the air war the cannon was responsible for destroying a number of Iraqi vehicles including 23 tanks destroyed in one day utilizing the cannon and Maverick air-to-ground missiles. (Jim Tunney)

Right: Art work on returning A-10s of the 23rd TFW consisted of decorated boarding ladder doors. For many years these doors have provided a perfect canvas for a variety of Warthog art work, COMBAT HAWG on 77-0133 is an excellent example. (Kevin Foy)

Far right: MUDDY, a boarding ladder door on an unidentified A-10 of the 23rd TFW. (Kevin Foy)

A-10A, 82-0653, MISFIT. (Kevin Foy)

A-10A, 80-0189, DEANO'S DAY IN THE SAND. (Kevin Foy)

A-10A, 82-0665, COOL CAT, THE LAST TIGER, an obvious reference to the fact that this A-10A was the last example to roll off the Fairchild assembly line. (Kevin Foy)

A-10A, 80-0178, MONGO. (Kevin Foy)

Right: A-10A, 80-0115, STAUD, this A-10A also displays the old style squadron markings of the 23rd Fighter Group. (Kevin Foy)

Left: Nearly each returning A-10 displayed some form of scoreboard. These markings, applied to an A-10 of the 23rd TFW, were typical of the mission markings displayed on many A-10s. Of interest are three MiG kills at the top - obviously destroyed on the ground. (Kevin Foy)

The OA-10A was introduced to combat by the 23rd TASS during the Gulf war. The unit flew some of the riskiest missions of the air war, subsequently suffering nearly half the A-10 losses incurred during the Gulf war. The designation OA-10 has more to do with the types mission as Forward Air Controller (FAC) than with any external differences between it and the A-10A. (Kevin Foy)

OA-10A, 77-0200, LIVE AND LET DIE. (Kevin Foy)

OA-10A, 77-0185, LENNI MAY. (Kevin Foy)

A-10A, 79-0182, FOR STORRMAN - WE'LL NEVER LET UP!, a reference to Capt. Richard D. Storr, a 23rd TFW pilot who was shot down and taken prisoner on 2 February 1991. (Kevin Foy)

A-10A, 79-0188, THE DECISIVE EDGE. (Kevin Foy)

A-10A, 80-0163, WE GIVE NO QUARTER. (Kevin Foy)

OA-10A, 76-0529, MARY JANE. (Kevin Foy)

Below: OA-10A, 77-0201, REGULATED TANG. (Kevin Foy)

Above right: OA-10A, 76-0537, ANGEL which features a unique adaptation of the Arizona state flag with the inscription BAD TO THE BONE. (Kevin Foy)

Right: OA-10A, 77-0163, WILD THING. Of interest is the additional art applied to the boarding ladder door, featuring Bart Simpson. (Kevin Foy)

OA-10A, 77-0270, MISS LYNN. (Kevin Foy)

OA-10A, 77-0209, ERIN O. Note the mission markings in the form of nails under the box containing the pilots name. Nails were used as mission markings since the 23rds callsign has been "Nail" since service during the war in Southeast Asia. (Kevin Foy)

OA-10A, 76-0547, THE UNKNOWN BOMBER. (Kevin Foy)

OA-10A, 77-0186, THE WARRIOR. (Kevin Foy)

Besides nose art, OA-10s of the 23rd TASS carried on the tradition of applying artwork to the boarding ladder door. Above and below are two examples are THE BOX SEAT on 77-0186, and Elmer Fudd with a 2.75 in. rocket slung over his shoulder on 77-0265. (Kevin Foy)

The 706th TFS/926th TFG, the only AFres combat unit to deploy to the Gulf did so during phase two of the Desert Shield build up. The unit made the fifteen hour flight from NAS New Orleans with the aid of KC-135s on hand to provide seven in-flight refuelings. (Jim Tunney)

A-10A of the 706th TFS in route home following the Gulf war. Of interest are the two 600 gallon long range external fuel tanks. (Jim Tunney)

OA-10A, 77-0208, PORKY'S REVENGE. (Kevin Foy)

OA-10A, 77-0190, ACES AND TEN'S ARE WILD. (Kevin Foy)

OA-10A, 77-0265, CHRISTINE. (Kevin Foy)

Above and right: A-10A, 76-0540, had a portion of its vertical stabilizer shot away during a combat sortie. Like its predecessor the P-47 Thunderbolt had done so many times during World War II, this Thunderbolt II brought its pilot home. Of interest is the "bandaid" applied to the tail. (Kevin Foy)

Left: A-10A, 77-0273, DESERT ROSE displays an impressive scoreboard and equally impressive art work. (Kevin Foy)

A-10A, 77-0274, NEW ORLEANS LADY. (Kevin Foy)

Patriotism and love of family is impressively displayed on A-10A, 77-0240. (Kevin Foy)

With the relationship between desert and camels, it was not long before 'Joe' the camel began to appear on aircraft taking part in Desert Shield/Desert Storm. He is seen here on A-10A, 77-0255 of the 706th TFS. (Kevin Foy)

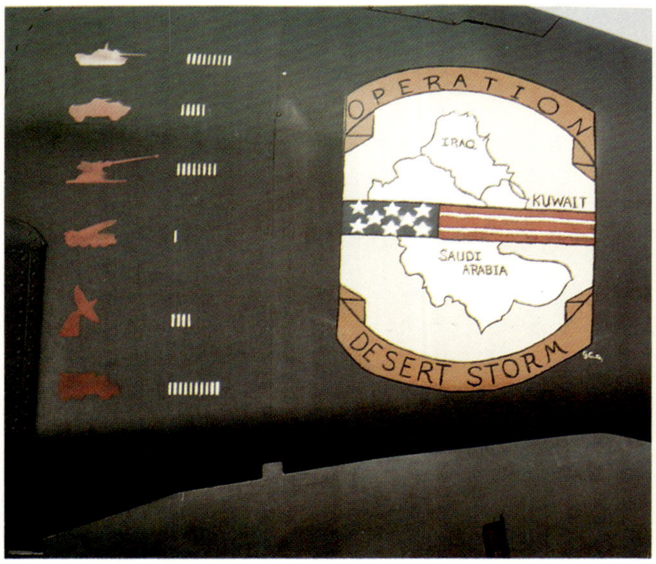

The 'official' Desert Storm patch was applied to A-10A, 77-0273. (Kevin Foy)

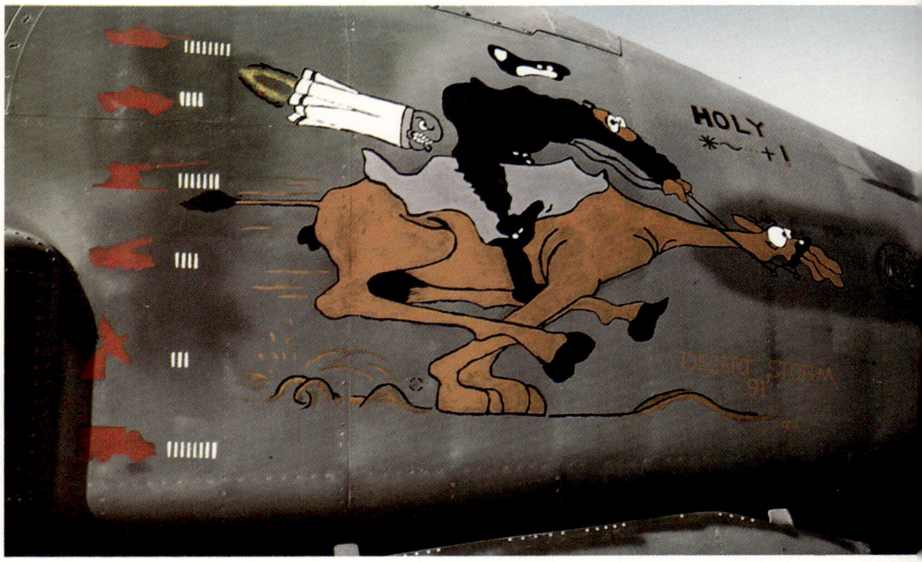

A-10, 77-0271, carries the second panel of a popular cartoon which made the rounds of copy machines during the war. The first panel featured an Iraqi warrior, on a charging camel screaming "Holy War." (Peter Wilson)

A-10A, 77-0260, FOUR LEAF CLOVER. (Kevin Foy)

ODIE, a character from the US comic strip Garfield, went to war on an A-10A of the 706th TFS, 77-0277. (Kevin Foy)

A crayfish (Crawdad) clutching a tank was applied to the left side of all 706th TFS A-10's. For the most part, nose art was carried on the right side. (Kevin Foy)

A-10A, 76-0544, DESERT STORM HEROES. (Kevin Foy)

A-10A, 77-0275, simply carries a boar's head. (Kevin Foy)

A-10A, 76-0531, STEPHANIE ANN. (Kevin Foy)

A-10A, 77-0269, BELLE OF NEW ORLEANS. (Kevin Foy)

On 6 February, 1991, Capt. Robert R. Swain Jr., was participating in an anti-armor sortie flying A-10A, 77-0205 of the 706th TFS. After delivering six 500-lb. bombs and two Mavericks, he observed two Iraqi helicopters skimming across the desert floor. Capt. Swain attempted to lock onto the choppers for a AIM-9 launch but was not successful. On his second pass he selected the 30mm cannon and turned one helicopter, a BO-105, into a pile of junk. (Kevin Foy)

A-10A, 77-0266, IRAQI NIGHTMARE. (Kevin Foy)

The 917th TFG, based at Barskdale AFB, contributed at least one A-10A to the war effort as an attrition replacement. The boar's head, consisting of eyes, ears and teeth is indicative of markings carried by the 917th TFG, AFres. (Kevin Foy)

A-10A, 77-0540, FIST. (Kevin Foy)

A-10A, 77-0268, CRESCENT CITY'S. The Warthog markings on the nose indicate this A-10A may have been an attrition replacement drawn from the 917th TFG, based at Barksdale AFB, LA. (Kevin Foy)

"Target rich environment" is the way one pilot described the KTO. On occasion the A-10's would run out of ordnance prior to running low on fuel. This A-10A of the 353rd TFS/354th TFW(P), has one remaining Maverick. Other wing stations are occupied by two AIM-9 Sidewinders and an AN/ALQ-119 ECM pod. (TSGT Rose Reynolds)

Below: Bart Simpson became a fixture on combat aircraft in the Gulf. Here, he rides a Rockeye cluster bomb on A-10A 79-0126 of the 353rd TFS. (Author)

A-10A's with nose art were the norm among the 354th TFW(P) Warthogs. Here, an unidentified artist begins to apply nose art to 78-0677, an A-10A of the 353rd TFS. (DOD)

Above right: A-10A, 78-0594, PANTHER PRINCESS, depicts . . . ah . . . female, riding a GAU-8 Avenger cannon. (Author)

Right: A-10A, 78-0667, INDIAN MAIDEN. (Kevin Foy)

Left and right: A-10A, 78-0681, clearly demonstrates how nose art changed. The first photograph was taken in the Gulf. The name LITTLE LADY DIANE appears on the side. The second photograph was taken shortly after the unit returned from the Gulf. Note the difference. (DOD - Right) (Author - Left)

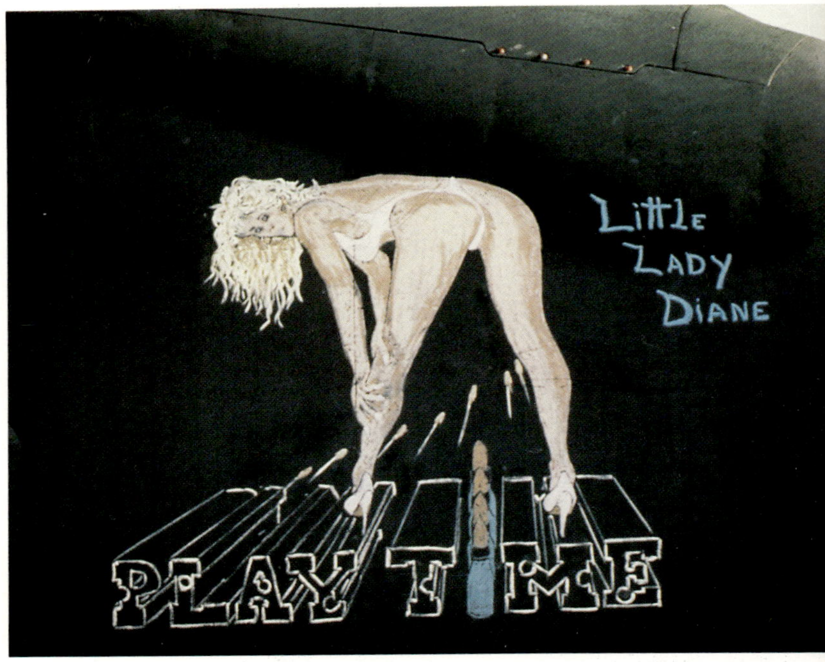

Below and right: A-10A, 79-0096, carried nose art on both sides. The left side was HONEY BUNS and the right WICKED SENSATION. (Author) (Kevin Foy)

Above: A-10A, 78-0664, VAL'S AVENGER. (Kevin Foy)

Left: A-10A, 78-0668, #1 TANK KILLER was just that, with 27 confirmed tank kills. This A-10 also destroyed 19 trucks, two radar sites, two APCs and one triple-A piece. (Author)

A-10A, 78-0680, VIEW TO A KILL featuring a scantily clad young lady riding a Maverick. (Kevin Foy)

A-10A, 78-0593, THE FORTUNE TEL_ER. (Author)

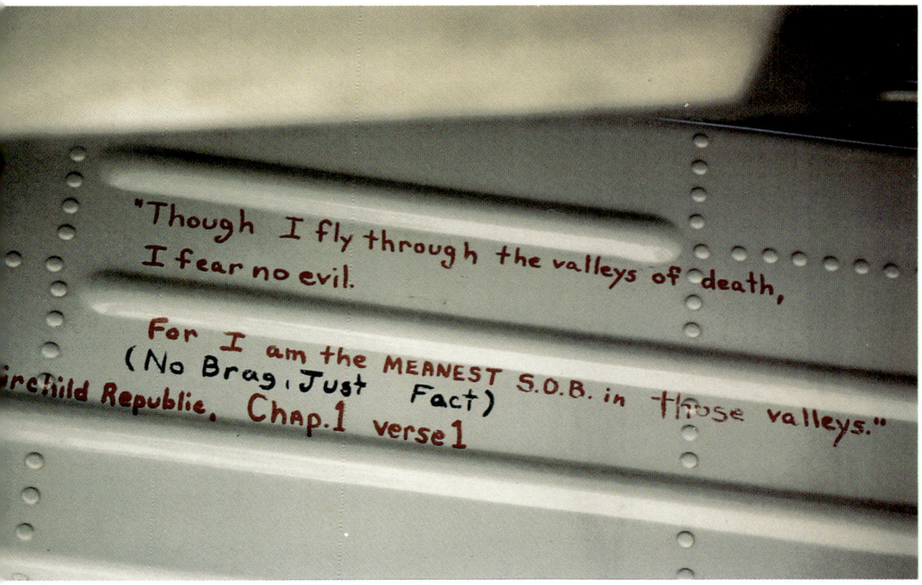

Above and below: A number of 354th TFW(P) A-10As carried mission markings inside the nose gear door as well as on its side. (Kevin Foy)

A-10A, 78-0595, RIP 'N TEAR. (Kevin Foy)

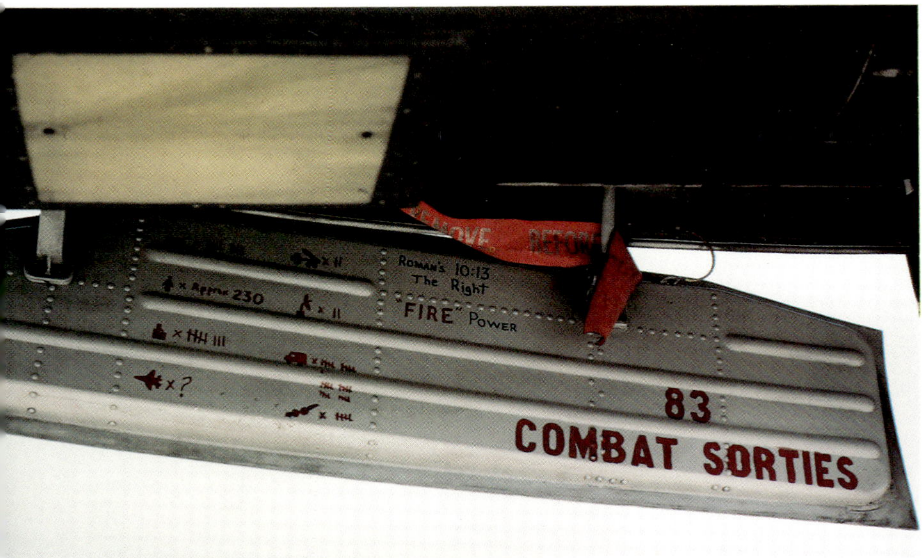

Right: A-10A, 79-0158, FALCON 1, commanders aircraft of the 355th TFS. (Kevin Foy)

Above: I doubt Walt Disney would have approved of this portrayal of Mickey Mouse on A-10A, 78-0686 of the 355th TFS. (Author)

Below: A-10A, 79-0099, FANG. (Author)

Above and below: A-10A, 78-0599, BIRD OF PREY featured a character from "Heckle and Jeckle", a U.S. comic strip. (Author - A-10) (Kevin Foy - Close up)

Above: Certainly many Iraqi troops regarded the A-10A as the GRIMREAPER. A-10A, 78-0665. (Author)

Right: A-10A, 78-0724, was another fine example of nose art applied to US tactical aircraft. Unfortunately it and other examples were ordered removed by the USAF shortly after these aircraft returned to the states. (Author)

Below: The significance of SHARPER THAN ANY TWO-EDGED SWORD, is not clear but the nose art on A-10A, 79-0163, is nevertheless eye catching. (Kevin Foy)

Cartoon character "Woody the Woodpecker" went to war with his SECRIT WEAPIN aboard A-10A, 78-0591. (Author)

A-10A, 79-0115, MUD BLOOD AND NO BEER, seems to sum up the mood of the maintenance troops who serviced and armed this Warthog. (Author)

Below: A-10A, 78-0603, KIMBERLY ANN. (Author)

A-10A, 78-0678, MIDNIGHT EXPRESS, bears nose art strikingly similar to that displayed on a P-51D, of the 487th Fighter Squadron during World War II. (Kevin Foy)

A-10A, 79-0173, THE FULL ARMOR OF GOD. (Kevin Foy)

A-10A, 78-0714, LOUISVILLE SLUGGER. (Kevin Foy)

GEORGIA GIRL, which adorned A-10A, 79-0100, is another example of tasteful art work applied to US aircraft. (Kevin Foy)

A glance at the pilots name, Capt. J. Wappner, explains why HERE COMES THE JUDGE was applied to his A-10A, 79-0112. Judge Wappner presides over a popular US television show, "Peoples Court." (Kevin Foy)

A-10A, 78-0622, FEAR NO EVIL. (Kevin Foy)

A-10A, 78-0592, BULLET EXPRESS. (Kevin Foy)

A-10A, 78-0654, KING OF PAIN. (Author)

A-10A, 78-0710, DARIN DAWNIE. (Kevin Foy)

A-10A, 79-0160, DOOBERS STING. (Kevin Foy)

“Sylvester the Cat”, was another popular US cartoon character which appeared on A-10A, 78-0662. “EAT THIS SADDAM”, appears quite appropriately on the side. (Kevin Foy)

A-10A, 79-0097, DAWG HAWG. (Kevin Foy)

As was the case with nearly every A-10A unit deployed to the Gulf, the 511th applied liberal amounts of mission markings and nose art to its A-10's. This example, DESERT BELLE, appeared on 81-0947. (John Grech)

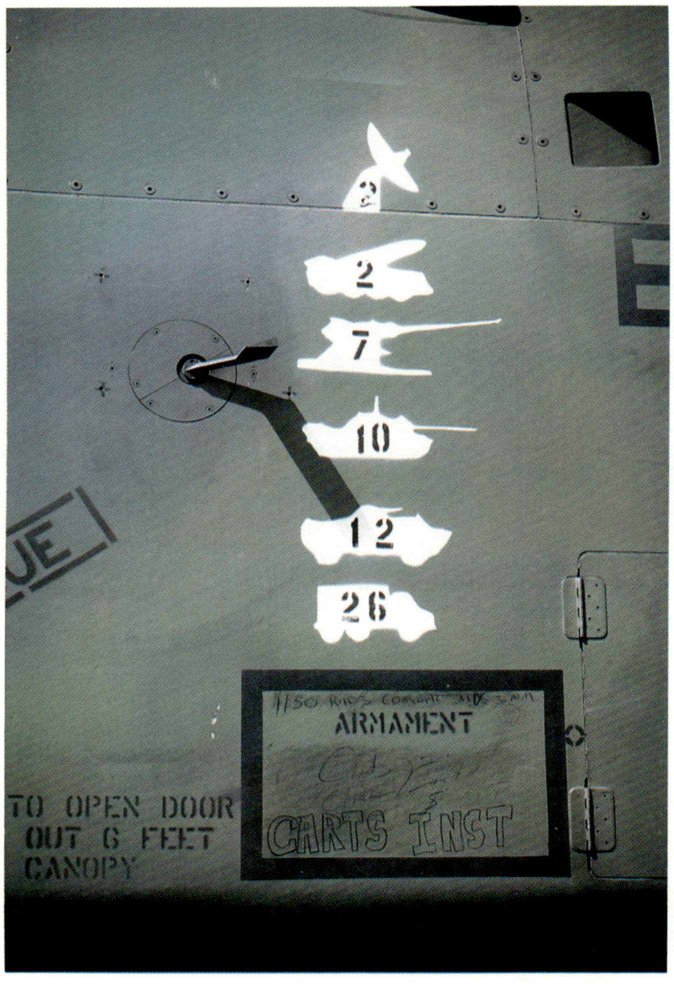

Right: Kill markings such as these were common on A-10A's of the 354th TFW (Provisional). (Author)

Left: The 511th TFS/10th TFW flew from RAF Alconbury and deployed to King Fahd IAP., Saudi Arabia. It was one of fifteen USAF squadrons dispatched to the Gulf from Europe. (Bob Archer)

This Phoenix was believed to be carried on A-10A, 80-0219. (John Grech)

A-10A, 80-0157, FIGHTING IRISH. (John Grech)

A-10A, 81-0979, depicts a bald eagle with a sub-machine gun. (John Grech)

A-10A, 79-0224, HAVE GUN WILL TRAVEL. (Bob Shane)

Above: LAKANUKI was an obvious play on syllables on A-10A, 80-0170. It is apparent the crew is referring to one of the lesser publicized shortages of the Gulf war. (John Grech)

Left: Another outstanding example of A-10A nose art was FREEDOM WAR-HOG, on 80-0194. (Andy Thomson)

A-10A, 81-0967, BROTHERS IN ARMS. (John Grech)

A-10A, 81-0948, HOG IN SPACE. (John Grech)

A-10A, 81-0990, WAR PIG. (John Grech)

A-10A, 81-0953, GIV'EM HELL! (Bob Shane)

A-10A, 79-0220, YANKEE EXPRESS. (Bob Shane)

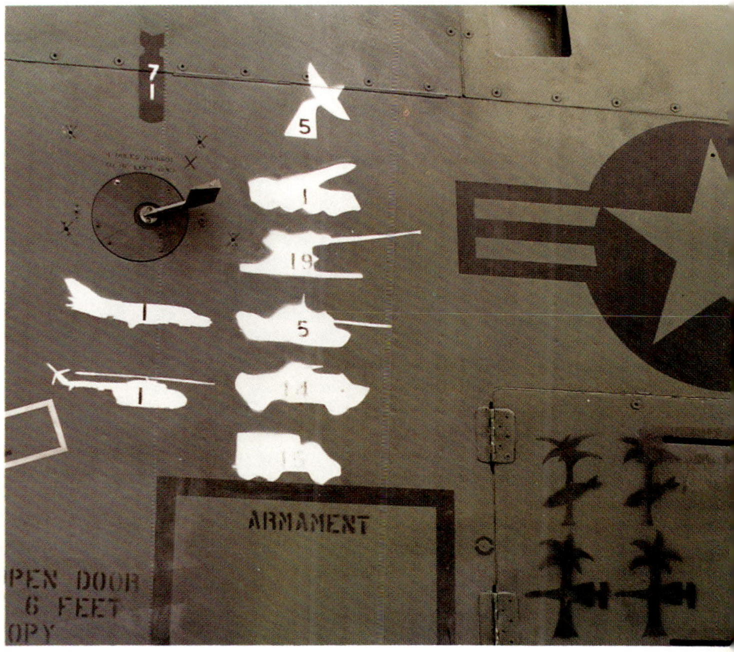

Above and left: "Dead-Heads" are everywhere, even in the Gulf during Desert Storm, as depicted by this Grateful Dead logo on 81-0964, STEAL YOUR FACE. This particular A-10 of the 511th TFS, scored the final aerial victory prior to the cease fire. On 15 February 1991, Capt. Todd "Shanghai" Sheehy used his GAU-8 Avenger cannon to destroy an Iraqi Mi-8 helicopter. (Bob Shane)

Below: Stars of Desert Storm one day and baking in the desert sun the next. Within months of returning from combat, this Gulf war veteran was relegated to an uncertain fate at the Aerospace Maintenance and Regeneration Center (AMARC), at Davis Monthan AFB, Arizona. (Bob Shane)

Below: ODIE, a character from the American comic strip "Garfield", uses an unconventional method of launching a Maverick missle. ODIE was displayed on A-10A, 80-0144, from the 511th TFS. (Bob Archer)

MCDONNELL DOUGLAS F-4 PHANTOM II

Even though the Phantom is rapidly nearing the end of its active service in the US it was deployed to the Gulf in sufficient numbers to form an all Phantom wing, the 35th TFW(Provisional). Based at Sheikh Isa, Bahrain, the wing included two F-4G Wild Weasel squadrons designed to hunt for and kill enemy SAM sites, and two squadrons of RF-4Cs drawn from the USAF and ANG.

At twenty-three years old, the F-4G Wild Weasel variant was considered one of the newest Phantoms in USAF service. Their motto, "First in, last out", was coined by F-105G Wild Weasel crews during the Vietnam war and still held true during Desert Storm. The F-4G went in ahead of the Strike Package patrolling along its route of travel. An Iraqi SAM site foolish enough to engage an F-4G or the Strike Package, soon discovered itself the target of a High Speed Anti-Radiation missile (HARM). The HARM, or AGM-88A, was utilized in conjunction with the Wild Weasels APR-47 radar attack and warning system which is capable of detecting, displaying, classifying and targeting functioning enemy radars. Once launched, the AGM-88 zeros in on a radar site even though the operator had shut it down. This leaves the SAMs without guidance from the ground, leaving them to be launched ballistically with far less accuracy. A total of 918 HARMs were launched by the 35th TFW(P). Without this vital asset, strike packages would have had to run a gauntlet of radar directed SAMs and AAA.

The 106th TRS/117th TRW, of the Alabama Air National Guard made up the first recce assets to arrive in Southwest Asia. These volunteers from the 106th brought along six LOROPs equipped RF-4Cs. LOROPs or LOng Range Oblique Photography system permitted the USAF to look deep into Iraq, as far as 55 miles while flying at altitudes approaching 30,000 feet. On the eve of the air campaign, the 117th departed the Gulf region but their LOROPs equipped Phantoms remained, flown by the 192nd TRS, Nevada Air National Guard. During phase two of the Desert Shield buildup, additional RF-4Cs, from the 67th TRW, Bergstrom AFB., Texas, and the 26th TRW, from Zeibrucken AB., Germany arrived in the Gulf region. During Desert Shield/Desert Storm, the venerable RF-4C proved invaluable, providing essential reconnaissance information to the Central Air Force high command.

Armed with a pair of HARMs, this F-4G Wild Weasel prepares to enter Iraqi air space to clear a corridor for a following strike package. (DOD)

Excellent air-to-air study of a pair of F-4Gs. Each strike package was accompanied by at least two Wild Weasels operating under the call sign of a popular brand of American beer, ie; STROH'S, MILLER etc. The pod mounted beneath the Phantom is an AN/ALQ-184 ECM pod. (Don Spering/AIR)

Left: The badge of the 35th TFW. (Author)

Right: HARM launch markings on an F-4G of the 81st TFS. (Bob Shane)

Col. James F. Brown, Commander of the 117th TRW, deployed to the Persian Gulf with six RF-4C's early in August 1990. At 53 years of age, he was one of the most experienced Phantom pilots to participate in Desert Shield. His LOROP equipped Phantoms were turned over to the 192nd TRS on the eve of the Gulf war. (Barry Roop)

An inglorious end to a glorious career. Like many other Gulf war veterans, this F-4G, of the 81st TFS, is about to begin its retirement at AMARC, Davis-Monthan AFB, AZ. (Bob Shane)

The 106th TRS commander's aircraft was flown to the Gulf as an attrition replacement for 64-1044 which was lost in a crash on 8 October 1990. This RF-4C was photographed after the war. Of interest is the AIM-9, as the RF-4C usually flies "alone and unarmed." (Barry Roop)

Right: Mission markings on the splitter plate of this 106th TRS, RF-4C indicate that it was active during Desert Storm. Each camel represents five missions. (Charles E. Mesker)

The LOROP system consists of a 66-in. focal length KS-127 camera and was quite capable of obtaining interpretable photography from very long ranges. Although no RF-4Cs were lost in combat, one example, 64-1044, crashed prior to Desert Storm and 64-1056 was lost following the conflict. Both were assigned to the 106th. (DOD)

Examples of Gulf war nose art on RF-4Cs consisted of cartoon-like characters such as "Joe" the camel, drawn with chalk or grease pencil. (Bryan Wilburn)

Markings on RF-4C, 69-0384, of the 12th TRS following its return to Bergstrom AFB. Note the addition of "Blackbirds" to the fin cap. (Mel Brown)

RECCE REBELS, on the nose of RF-4C 64-0843, the 106th TRS commanders aircraft. The medium appears to be chalk and or grease pencil. (Charles Mesker)

The 192nd TRS, deployed at least one RF-4C to the Persian Gulf as an attrition replacement. Photographed after the war with a shark's mouth. It is doubtful it flew combat missions with this art work since all such markings were ordered removed from 35th TFW(P) aircraft on the eve of Desert Storm. (Mike Grove)

This 12th TRS RF-4C was photographed at Bergstrom AFB, during the every stages of Desert Shield. Prior to combat, all high visibility markings were removed to conform with other 35th TFW(P) Phantoms. Even wing, squadron and command badges were painted out. Following the conflict, these markings were reapplied. (Author)

During phase two of the Desert Shield build up, the final two active Air Force RF-4C units deployed aircraft to the Gulf. The 26th TRW was assigned to the 7440th Provisional Wing in Turkey. The 67th TRW deployed RF-4C's from Bergstrom AFB, TX on 9 January 1991, becoming a key element of the 35th TFW(P) at Sheikh Isa AB, Bahrain. (Barry Roop)

GENERAL DYNAMICS F-16 FALCON

Though the F-16 is officially known as the Fighting Falcon, those who fly and fix it prefer to call it the "Viper" or "Electric Jet." Those who do not, refer to it as the "Lawn Dart." During the Gulf war the F-16 earned yet another name, "Killer Bee." After attacking strategic targets around Baghdad during the first week of the war, the eleven squadrons of F-16s deployed to the Gulf literally swarmed over Iraq and the KTO. This impressive force of F-16s was controlled by FACs, (OA-10s, F/A-18Ds or F-16Cs), which quite literally acted as traffic cops directing F-16s to various targets within 10 mile by 10 mile "kill boxes." Combat loads normally consisted of two external fuel tanks, AN/ALQ-119 or 131 ECM pod, four AIM-9 Sidewinders (later reduced to two), 500-lb. and 1000-lb. low drag bombs, CBUs and Mavericks. (The TMD, ammunition which dispenses anti-armor and personnel mines was also delivered by F-16s.)

This F-16C was assigned to the 17th TFS as an attrition replacement aircraft. The 'DS' tailcode has been reported to mean 'Designated Spare' or 'Desert Storm'. The fin cap colors represent the three Falcons squadrons, 10th 17th and 33rd which were assigned to the 363rd TFW(P). (Author)

Above: The 17th TFS returned home with some very interesting art work. Unfortunately, it suffered the same fate as other examples and was removed within weeks of returning home. 'BLOOD STORM' on F-16C, 84-1261, was a perfect example of this nose art. (Author)

Impressive tally of mission markings applied to a 17th TFS, F-16C, 84-1262. On many F-16C's this scoreboard was continued on both sides of the canopy. (Kevin Foy)

Loaded with CBU's and an AN/ALQ-119 ECM pod, F-16Cs of the 17th and 10th TFS fly formation with a KC-135 while conducting aerial refueling. (DOD)

A 17th TFS, F-16C pulls away from a KC-135 following refueling. Of interest is the absence of Sidewinders indicating that this photo was taken late in the air campaign following the achievement of air supremacy. (DOD)

F-16C, 83-1153, "Batman." (Author)

F-16C, 84-1215, "FOSTER'S EXPRESS." (Author)

Cartoon trouble maker Bart Simpson went to war aboard F-16C, 84-1244, "Eat My Shorts Hussein." (Author)

F-16C, 84-1257, "DESERT STORM", depicts a weather map of Iraq covered with a hurricane. (Author)

HERE HUSSEIN SURPRISE, displayed on 83-1165, represents two cartoon characters, one the ruler of Iraq and the other from the American comic strip "BC." (Author)

F-16C, 84-1254, NEXT, another work of art fitting for the role played by the Falcon during the Gulf war. (Author)

F-16C, 84-1213, TAZMANIAN DEVIL. (Author)

F-16C, 83-1145, "DEATH DEALER." All F-16 art work was applied with either chalk or grease pencil and was not permanent. (Author)

This beauty appearing on F-16C, 84-1241, HOOTER'S STANDARDS is indicative of the high standards demanded by the 'Hoot Owls' of the 17th TFS. (Author)

F-16C, 84-1256, NIGHT STALKER. (Author)

F-16C, 84-1247, WAR WENCH.(Author)

Above and right: When an aircraft is "Code One" it can be returned to flight quickly. The F-16 returned Code One from many sorties, 85-1420, more so than others. (Author)

SSgt Warren D. Trask, deployed to the gulf as a member of the 19th TFS/363rd TFW. During Desert Shield Desert Storm he was assigned to the 33rd TFS and was responsible for applying some of the best artwork to emerge from the war on that squadrons aircraft. (Author)

Another reference to a particular F-16 in the squadron, SWEET BUT DEADLY on 83-1158. (Kevin Foy)

Right: F-16C, 84-1219, HOT COCK, which stands for an aircraft with all systems aligned and ready for immediate flight. The reclining gamecock is a tribute to the maintenance troops of the 19th TFS, the Gamecocks, which deployed to augment the 17th and 33rd TFS. (Author)

F-16C, 84-1381, HAMMER TIME, featuring "JACKHAMMER JENNY" riding a bomb ala actor Slim Pickins in the movie "Dr. Strangelove." (Author)

F-16C, 83-1150, MAX THRUST. The pilot wanted a couple of typical Texas beauties applied to his aircraft with F-16s demonstrating how fast they can get in and out, hence the circling Falcons. (Author)

F-16C, 83-1142, HARMFUL FX, a reference to special effects. The helpless lass represents Kuwait and of course, the "Rambo" figure, the U.S. coming to her rescue. (Author)

Above: "Desert Shield" appeared on 85-1419, the Wing Commander's F-16C. This particular work of art was quite possibly the most detailed depiction attempted by Sgt. Trask. SSgt Trask professed to having no formal art training, and his medium consisted only of GI issue grease pencils. (Author)

F-16C, 84-1240, WILD THANG, artist unknown. (Author)

Above and right: 10th TFS F-16C returns to its European base at Hahn AB, Germany. AMU stands for Aircraft Maintenance Unit. Of interest is the nose art and name SABRE ONE which denotes this aircraft as belonging to the squadron commander. (Marc Brouyere)

Above: Nose art on F-16C, 84-1267, FEEL LUCKY? (DOD)

Above right: F-16C, serial 84-1267, FEEL LUCKY? of the 10th TFS/ 50th TFW, returns to Hahn AB, Germany following Operation Desert Storm. Note that this aircraft is carrying live AIM-9 Sidewinders and an ACM pod. (Marc Brouyere)

F-16C, 84-1265, WILD CHILD, featuring "Spaceman Spiff" from the Calvin and Hobbes comic strip. (Author)

The 401st TFW, Torrejon AB. Spain, deployed two squadrons of F-16's to support Desert Shield/Desert Storm. The 614th established the 401st TFW(P) at Doha AB, Qatar. The 612th, joined the 7440th Provisional Wing at Incirlik Turkey. (Scott Snell)

An F-16C, of the 614th TFS, lifts off the runway at Doha AB. It carries a typical load for Gulf war Falcons, four AIM-9s, CBUs and a AL/ANQ-131 self-protection jammer pod. (Michael P. Kopack Jr.)

F-16C, 87-0257, of the 614th TFS, was lost on 20 January 1991. Its pilot, Capt. Harry M. Roberts was captured and released following the war. (Scott Snell)

Banking in the refueling track with a KC-135, two F-16C's from the 614th TFS prepare to enter Iraqi airspace with a load of 500-lb. low drag bombs and CBUs. (DOD)

Waiting for another call from an F-16C "FASTFAC", two 614th TFS Falcons patrol the KTO. The wingman has expended his CBUs, while lead still retains a 1000-lb low drag bomb. (DOD)

The 388th TFW has been operating the F-16 Falcon longer than any operational unit in the world. They brought their expertise and two squadrons of the latest F-16Cs to the Gulf, forming the 388th TFW(Provisional) at Al Minhad AB, UAE.

Right: F-16Cs, from the 388th TFW served as FASTFACs for other Coalition aircraft. As such they would patrol "kill boxes" pinpointing targets and directing aircraft in for the kill. (DOD)

Above and right: The 69th TFS/347th TFW, also deployed to the Gulf. Assigned to the 388th TFW(P), the 69th took part in the Scud hunts alongside other Coalition aircraft. Mission markings on the nose gear door consist of a camel in a cross-hairs and a "Scud Busters" patch. (Kevin Foy, both)

AN/AAQ-13 Navigation pod carried on the port side of F-16Cs serving as FASTFACs during the Gulf war. (Author)

Above and right: The time honored tradition of applying graffiti to bombs was kept alive during Desert Storm as attested to by these CBUs and iron bombs hung from F-16s of various units. (via Lou Drendel)

Below and below right: Soft skinned vehicles like this SA-3 (GOA), truck reload system and SA-6 (Gainful) surface to air missile system were quite susceptible to CBU's delivered by F-16s. (DOD)

GENERAL DYNAMICS F-111 AARDVARK

A total of 64 F-111E/F's and 18 EF-111A's from six squadrons were deployed during the build up known as Desert Shield. The majority of the deployment consisted of F-111F's from the 48th TFW which established itself as a provisional wing at Taif AB, Saudi Arabia. The wing was further strengthened with the arrival of two detachments of EF-111A Ravens from the 390th ECS/366th TFW and the 42nd ECS/66th ECW.

Flying their missions at night and utilizing its AVQ-26 Pave Tack FLIR Target Acquisition and Laser designating pod, the F-111F proved to be devastatingly effective against hardened shelters, bridges, tanks and other armored vehicles. Iraqi tank crews were unaware they were under attack until their tank blew up. One captured Iraqi General summed it up well, "During the Iran war, my tank was my friend . . . During this war my tank became my enemy . . . None of my troops would get near a tank at night because they kept blowing up." By the end of the air campaign, F-111Fs of the 48th TFW(P) had accounted for 920 Iraqi armored vehicles.

48th TFW(P) strike packages consisted of F-111F Aardvarks and EF-111A Ravens or 'Sparkvarks' as they are popularly known. The commonality of the strike force was a result of the F-111s unique flying characteristics and high dash speeds. Although the EF-111A was quite capable of 'whiting-out' Iraqi radar, the strike package, at times was supported by HARM shooting F-4Gs, and, of course, the F-15C which was ever present providing Combat Air Patrol. Precision Guided Munitions (PGM) were employed on the majority of missions. The most famous use of such ordnance took place on 26/27 January 1991, when F-111F's of the 48th TFW(P) used GBU-15 Glide Bombs to knock out two pumping stations dumping millions of gallons of crude oil into the Persian Gulf. Aside from the F-15E Strike Eagle, the F-111F was the only USAF type capable of launching the GBU-15.

F-111F, of the 494th TFS returns from a mission with empty wing stores with the exception of two CBU's. (DOD)

Although a typical F-111 strike might include as many as 53 aircraft, targets were struck by single aircraft spaced one or more minutes apart. These 48th TFW(P) F-111F's are participating in a daylight training mission during Desert Shield. Nearly all F-111F attacks were conducted at night. (DOD)

Although the 495th TFS/48th TFW, did not deploy to the Gulf, a handful of its aircraft and crews did. This F-111F represents the 495th TFS, commanders aircraft. It carries three rows of mission markings under the windscreen. (Andy Thomson)

One of the first aerial victories of the war involved an unarmed EF-111A, 66-0016, from the 42nd ECS/66th ECW. While flying its first mission of the war, it was attacked by an Iraqi Mirage F.1. Unable to match the EF-111, the Iraqi pilot literally flew into the ground. Since this engagement also involved an F-15C from the 58th TFS, piloted by Capt. Robert E. Graeter, credit for the Mirage kill was given to him. (Evidence supplied by an AWACS monitoring the fight confirmed the decision to award the kill to Graeter). (Roberto Zambon)

The commonality between the F-111 and the EF-111 allowed it to race low across the desert with the strike package, jamming Iraqi radars along the way. This example is from 390th ECS/366th TFW. (Brian C. Rogers)

LOCKHEED F-117 NIGHTHAWK

The people of Southwest Asia called it 'Shabba' or ghost. The news media referred to it as the Stealth Fighter. Those who flew and maintained it called it the 'Blackjet.' Unofficially, it was the Nighthawk, a product of the legendary Lockheed "Skunk Works", and an outgrowth of a 1977 black program known as "Have Blue." The Nighthawk, or Blackjet, was unveiled on 21 April 1990 at Nellis AFB, NV. Operational long before its existence was ever acknowledged, the F-117 entered USAF service with the 4450th Tactical Group in October, 1983. Its combat debut arrived on 19 December 1989, when a flight of four penetrated Panamanian airspace and bombed a barracks complex during Operation Just Cause.

On 19/20 August 1990, twenty F-117A's of the 415th TFS/37th TFW, deployed to Khamis Mushait AB. Situated in the south Arabian peninsula, the new base was quickly dubbed "Tonopah East." This initial deployment was followed by additional F-117's from the 416th TFS and a detachment of aircraft and pilots from the 417th TFTS. On the eve of Desert Storm, 45 Blackjets were on hand to participate in the opening phase of the air campaign.

At 0230 hours, local, on 17 January 1991, F-117s began to drop away from their KC-135's heading for high value heavily defended targets in and around Baghdad. On that first night the F-117 took out several strategic targets including a key telecommunications building and headquarters for the Iraqi Air Force. Ordnance consisted primarily of 2000-lb, GBU-10 and GBU-27 laser guided bombs. At least one target, the Iraqi Air Force headquarters, was attacked with a deep penetration GBU-27 laser guided bomb. Through the course of the air war, the Blackjet flew 1,271 combat sorties, all under cover of darkness, and without loss.

Interesting view of an F-117A showing the 'platypus' exhaust arrangement designed to reduce the heat signature of the Nighthawk. (DOD)

Although its design is state-of-the-art, many of the components of the F-117 were borrowed from other aircraft. The navigation system from the B-52, the cockpit is a combination of systems from the F-16 and F/A-18 and its environmental control systems are from the C-130. Of interest is the lack of conventional flaps on the F-117 resulting in it landing "hot", at approximately 175 kts. (Barry Roop)

Right: Looking very much like an arrow, the F-117 is described as being very nimble in the air. (Barry Roop)

Below: F-117A post flight checks performed at Khamis Mushait AB, Saudi Arabia. Of interest are the open weapons bay doors. In order to reduce its radar signature, the F-117 carries its ordnance, usually a pair of 2000-lb laser guided bombs, internally. (DOD)

Mission markings typical to F-117s returning from the Gulf. (Barry Roop)

F-117A, 85-0814, "FINAL VERDICT." (Bob Shane)

Barely visible on the weapons bay door of F-117A, 85-0813, is artwork and the name "THE TOXIC AVENGER." (Bob Shane)

F-117 Nighthawk of the 37th TFW, taxis out for a daylight training sortie. Barely visible on the vertical stabilizer is the "TR" code of the 37th, signifying its permanent base at the Tonopah Test Range, in Nevada. Following the Gulf war, the three Nighthawk squadrons moved to Holloman AFB, N.M. becoming the 49th FW. (DOD)

F-117A, Nighthawk of the 37th TFW, awaits its next nocturnal mission. The pile of stones behind the Nighthawk is actually the roof of a hardened shelter. The 37th moved into brand-new facilities at Khamis Mushait AB, Saudi Arabia during Operation Desert Shield. (DOD)

SPECIAL OPERATIONS

The Air Force Special Operations Command was established 22 May 1990, at Hurlburt Field, FL. Its role is to organize, train, equip and educate Air Force special operations forces for worldwide deployment. The command undertook just such a deployment when practically the entire 1st Special Operations Wing moved from Hurlburt Field to King Fahd International Airport, Saudi Arabia. The wing began Psychological Warfare Operations in November by broadcasting 'Voice of America' into the KTO and Iraq. These were followed by mass leaflet drops which continued throughout Desert Storm. On 14 January 1991, elements of the 1st SOW were forward deployed to Al Jouf AB, in western Saudi Arabia near the Iraq border.

On 17 January 1991, at 0228 hours Saudi time, a pair of 20th SOS Pave Low III helicopters became the first Coalition aircraft to enter Iraqi airspace as they guided AH-64 Apache helicopters as part of Task Force Normandy. This strike force was successful in knocking out Iraqi early warning radars, thus opening a corridor for Coalition air forces. Throughout the remainder of the conflict, the 1st SOW participated in Combat SAR, Close Air Support and infiltration/exfiltration missions into the KTO and Iraq.

The MH-53J Pave Low III is the most technologically advanced helicopter in the world and the largest and most powerful helicopter in the USAF inventory. During Desert Storm, an MH-53J made a successful recovery of a downed Navy pilot over 100 miles inside Iraq. (DOD)

On 3 February 1991, the first of eleven 15,000-lb, BLU-82 bombs was delivered by an 8th SOS, MC-130E Combat Talon. These huge bombs were palletized and the entire package was pushed out the rear loading door. The BLU-82 was intended to clear mines and break the will of Iraqi troops. Of interest is the M904 fuse extender and the greetings applied to the bomb. (Norb Feist)

Below: The 9th SOS operated the HC-130N/P in the Gulf theatre as an air refueling platform for Special Operations helicopters. Also known as Combat Shadow, the HC-130, participated in the dropping of more than 25 million leaflets urging Iraqis to surrender. (DOD)

The MH-60G, Pave Hawks of the 55th SOS/1st SOW, made their combat debut during Desert Storm. A highly modified version of the Sikorsky Blackhawk, the Pave Hawk's equipped with FLIR, terrain avoidance radar and a in-flight refueling receptacle. These upgrades made it an ideal candidate for special operations at night and in marginal weather. (DOD)

On 21 January 1991, an MH-53J of the 20th SOS rescued Lt. Devon Jones, F-14A(Plus) pilot shot down deep in Iraqi territory. The rescue was supported by two 353rd TFS A-10s which spent a total of eight hours in the air. (Norb Feist)

The MC-130E Combat Talon, is a highly modified C-130 Hercules equipped with aerial refueling, terrain following and avoidance radar, an inertial navigation system and the Fulton surface to air recovery system. During Desert Storm the type was used to refuel special operations helicopters and infiltration and exfiltration of Special Operations forces. (DOD)

Graphic representation of the Spectre emblem on an AC-130H of the 16th SOS. (DOD)

Left: The sign reads "GHOST RIDER INN", indicating it is inhabited by members of the 16th Special Operations Squadron, flying AC-130Hs from King Fahd IAP, Saudi Arabia. (Norb Feist)

Right: Examples of munitions fired by the 105mm howitzer and 40mm Bofars used by the AC-130H. (Norb Feist)

The 193rd Special Operations Group, Pennsylvania Air National Guard, deployed the EC-130 to the Gulf. The EC-130E(RR), 'Rivet Rider.' During Desert Shield, commencing in November, 1990, EC-130's began to beam 'Voice of America' into Iraq and the KTO. During Desert Storm, the units EC-130E's were airborne broadcast stations urging Iraqi troops to surrender, which they did by the thousands. During one such mission, an EC-130E of the 193rd SOG, stayed aloft for 21 hours setting a new C-130 record for refueled flight time. (Author)

Five AC-130H Spectre Gunships of the 16th SOS deployed to the Gulf in September, 1990. During the war they were utilized to provide close air support. On one such mission, supporting besieged Maries pinned down near Khafji, AC-130H, 69-6567, was struck by a surface-to-air missile and crashed into the Gulf, killing all aboard. (DOD)

HH-3 Jolly Green Giant helicopters of the 71st SOG, AFres, arrived in the Gulf 12 January 1991. The type flew a number of reconnaissance missions from King Fahd IAP, Saudi Arabia. (Bob Shane)

The Incirlik wing possessed two F-15C squadrons, of the 525th TFS and 32nd TFS. These two squadrons downed a total of fourteen Iraqi aircraft, including three aircraft which violated the post war ban on flight by Iraqi fixed wing aircraft. This F-15C is from the 525th TFS 36th TFW. (Marc Brouyere)

On 19 January 1991, Lt. David G. Svenden, of the 32nd TFS/32nd TFW, used an AIM-7 Sparrow to down an Iraqi F.1EQ. He was flying F-15C, 79-0021 at the time. Unfortunately, F-15Cs were not present in sufficient strength to provide around-the-clock combat air patrol over northern Iraq. Consequently, a number of Iraqi aircraft were able to seek refuge in neighboring Iran. (Alex Knoops)

The 401st TFW deployed one squadron, the 612th TFS, to support the 7440th Provisional Wing. Another squadron, the 614th, also flying F-16C's, was deployed to Doha AB, Qatar. (Scott Snell)

F-4G, 69-0244, NIGHT STALKER of the 23rd TFS/ 52nd TFW, displays Phantom characters as mission markings. The Wild Weasels from the 23rd TFS worked in conjunction with HARM launching F-16C/Ds to suppress Iraqi SAM sites. (Bob Archer)

F-16C/Ds of the 23rd TFS/52nd TFW, launched AGM-45 Strikes and AGM-88 HARMs in support of F-4G missions. (Marc Brouyere)

Mission markings in the form of small Falcon stencils were typical on 23rd TFS F-16C/D's. (Kevin Foy)

Had the war lasted longer, there is little doubt that these TISEO and Pave Tack equipped F-4E's of the 3rd TFS/3rd TFW, would have become actively involved illuminating targets for other aircraft carrying laser guided ordnance. (Barry Roop)

As Operation Desert Shield was going into high gear, the 26th TRW was at Bergstrom AFB hoping to repeat as winners of the Reconnaissance Air Meet. The unit then deployed to Incirlik AB, Turkey to form the recce assets of the 7440th Wing. Shortly after the war, the unit was disbanded and its RF-4Cs delivered to AMARC at Davis-Monthan AFB, AZ. (Bob Shane)

Right and below: The 66th ECW, deployed two electronic warfare aircraft to support the 7440th Wing, the EF-111A Raven of the 42nd ECS, and the EC-130H Compass Call Hercules of the 43rd ECS. Both types supported strike packages by providing close-in and stand-off jamming of Iraqi radar and communication systems. (DOD - EF-111) (Authors collection - EC-130)

The 77th TFS/20th TFW, was conducting weapons training at Incirlik AB, when Iraq invaded Kuwait. The squadron remained in Turkey and was later joined by another F-111E equipped unit the 79th TFS. Initially, the two squadrons attacked at low level, supported by EF-111A's and Wild Weasels. The Iraqi air defense threat forced them to conduct attacks from a much higher altitude. Lacking the Pave Tack system of the F-111F, the 77th and 79th TFS attacked under cover of darkness delivering CBU-87 or 89 Cluster bombs. (Andy Thomson)

Forming an integral part of the 7440th Wing, were three E-3B/C Sentrys of the 552nd Airborne Command and Control Wing. Better known as the AWACs, the E-3 was capable of alerting Combat Air Patrol aircraft the instant an Iraqi aircraft left the ground. (DOD)

Mission markings on an F-111E of the 20th TFW. (John Grech)

E-3Cs were instrumental in directing F-15s to airborne threats. Three Iraqi flags have been applied to E-3C, 82-0006, of the 552nd ACCW signifying F-15C aerial victories over MiG-23s. (Bob Archer)

A holdover from the Vietnam war, the AC-130A was possibly making its final combat appearance. The 711th SOS/919th SOG, provided six AC-130As in support of the 7440th Wing. (Author)

AC-130A, 55-0014, carries the Spectre insignia and rows of camels signifying missions flown. This particular Sperectre gunship was named JAWS OF DEATH. The bulge on the side of this AC-130A is the 'Black Crow' Direction Finder radar tuned to detect the frequency of motor vehicle ignition systems. (Author)

Left: Although C-130A, 56-0522, carries the Spectre insignia, it is not a gunship. However, it did support the 711th SOS during the war transporting high priority cargo and personnel to and from the Gulf. (Author)

AC-130A, 53-3129, FIRST LADY, denotes the fact that this aircraft is the first production C-130A built. It is not clear whether the FIRST LADY flew combat missions during Desert Storm. (Author)

MILITARY AIRLIFT COMMAND

During Desert Shield/Desert Storm, 90% of the C-5 Galaxy fleet and 80% of the C-141 Starlifter fleet was utilized moving men and material to Southwest Asia. Three-quarters of the cargo and one-third of the personnel airlifted to the Gulf arrived on either C-5's or C-141's. Every airlift squadron in the USAF, ANG and AFres was involved, either providing aircrews, aircraft or both. In addition, the government activated the Civil Reserve Air Fleet (CRAF) for the first time in its 38-year history. The total number of civilian airliners and cargo aircraft available for military use eventually reached 158 during Desert Storm. Sixteen different airfields were receiving 8,000 troops daily. At the height of Desert Storm, a transport aircraft was landing every 11 minutes.

Once reaching the Gulf Theatre, cargo and personnel were moved intra-theatre by a fleet of perhaps as many as 200 C-130E/H Hercules from at least fifteen tactical airlift squadrons. Vital to the success of the ground war, Hercules were operating in and out of crude airstrips cut into the desert delivering 14,000 troops, 9,000 tons of cargo while flying 1,200 sorties.

MAC

In addition to the Hercules, intra-theatre transportation was provided by a host of lesser known but nevertheless invaluable aircraft such as the C-12, C-20, C-21, and C-22s of the Air National Guard. The C-21 proved to be a valuable asset providing a rapid means of transportation for reconnaissance imagery and the daily Air Tasking Orders. The C-12, C-20 and C-22 were instrumental in moving VIPs and senior Department of Defense officials throughout the Gulf region.

Art work did not appear on many MAC aircraft. However, it was abundant on C-130s operating within the theatre. Most C-130 nose art disappeared before these aircraft deployed back to the states. Here are a few examples of nose art displayed during the war and upon their return home.

DESERT WARRIOR, C-130E, 64-0537, from the 317th TAW. (Bob Mullendore via Keith Snyder)

C-130H, 85-1362, SNOOPY from the 136th TAW/181st TAS, Texas Air National Guard. (Keith Snyder)

C-130E, 68-10935, ROGER RABBIT, of the 435th TAW. (DOD)

C-130E, Hercules of the 327th TAS/913th TAG, AFres. It was photographed upon its return to NAS Willow Grove, PA. (Barry Roop)

Right: C-130E, 64-18240, PAYBACK TIME, of the 435th TAW. (DOD)

DESERT PHOENIX appeared in chalk on this Hercules of an unknown airlift squadron. (DOD)

C-130E, 70-1274, depicts a bull dog chewing up Iraq. (DOD)

Below: C-130E, 62-1803, from the 327th TAG/63rd TAS, AFres which is based at Selfridge ANGB, Michigan. (Jeff Rankin-Lowe/Sirius)

Right and below: DC-8 of Hawaiian Air and 747 from America West airlines represented a fraction of the 100 civil airliners called to service as part of the Civil Air Reserve Fleet. Of interest is the yellow ribbon and name FREEDOM BIRD, applied to the 747. (Author - DC-8) (DOD - 747)

"Yosemite Sam" delivers a message to Saddam Hussein via a C-130 during Operation Desert Shield. (CMSgt. Don Sutherland)

C-5A, of the 105th MAG/137th MAS lifts off on another Desert Storm supply mission. This unit of the NY ANG was heavily committed to the Gulf from August 1990 through March 1991. (Author)

Reserve airlift squadrons moved more than 235,000 troops and 454,000 tons of cargo. This C-141B, was rushed into service directly from a major overhaul and carries no unit markings. (Bob Archer)

Over 90% of the C-5 Galaxy fleet took part in moving material and personnel to the Gulf region. The entire tonnage moved during the Berlin airlift was exceeded by C-5's in the first six weeks of Desert Shield. One C-5A, 68-0228, of the 60th MAW was lost on 29 August 1990, at Ramstein AB. (DOD)

Below: C-130E, 63-7776, ARKANSAS DREAMIN', of the 314th TAW, took part in Operation Provide Comfort as evidenced by artwork on its nose. The 314th also took part in Operation Desert Storm. (Bob Shane)

Left: This lone camel appeared as a mission marking on a District of Columbia Air National Guard C-22. (Author)

Right and below: High priority cargo, VIPs, and high ranking officials were transported by a variety of aircraft including the C-21A Learjet, C-20B Gulfstream, and C-22. (Author)

Fortunately, C-9A Nightingales were not utilized at the rate many anticipated prior to the war. (DOD)

C-29A, of the 167th Flight Checking Squadron, was deployed to the Gulf to inspect and test fixed navigation systems at various air fields in the region. (Keith Snyder)

Typical y, U-2R and TR-1A missions were flown in excess of 60,000 feet lasting as long as nine hours. (DOD)

TR-1A's deployed to the Gulf flew with an experimental electro-optical system which enabled the transmission of near real time imagery. The long nose of this TR-1A carries the Advanced Synthetic Aperture Radar System (ASARS). The underwing Special Mission Pods, can contain a number of reconnaissance systems, in this case, Side Looking Airborne Radar, (SLAR). (John Grech)

TR-1A, 80-1081, 9th SRS/17th SRW. (John Grech)

Left: TR-1A, 80-1081, 9th SRS/17th SRW. (Andy Thomson)

TR-1A, 80-1089, 99th SRS/9th SRW. (Author)

U-2R, 80-1098, 99th SRS/9th SRW. (Author)

TR-1A, 80-1088, 9th SRS/17th SRW. (DOD)

STRATEGIC AIR COMMAND

The key to success in Desert Shield/Desert Storm was the role played by the KC-10A Extender and the KC-135 Stratotanker air-to-air refuelers. Approximately 200 KC-135's and 30 KC-10's were assigned to various Provisional Air Refueling Wings established in the Gulf region. Other tankers served to shuttle aircraft, personnel and cargo to the Gulf from the USA and Europe. A total of 34,000 refueling sorties were flown during Desert Shield/Desert Storm. This total includes some flown into Iraqi airspace to save strike aircraft dangerously low on fuel. Regardless of how fast, how high, or how low an aircraft could fly, or how stealthy it was, it still required tanker gas to "kick ass"!

Drawing from the entire B-52G fleet and supplementing crews with personnel selected from four B-52H units, the BUFF, as it is popularly known, flew 1,624 combat missions, delivering 25,700 tons of ordinance. Munitions consisted of MK-82 500-lb bombs, CBU-58 and 87 cluster bombs and the ordnance of choice, the 750-lb, M-117. Depending upon configuration, a B-52G could haul as many as fifty-one of these iron bombs. Although no match for precision guided munitions, a cell of three B-52Gs could leave a trail of destruction one mile wide and over a mile long.

Missions were launched from Moron AB, Spain, RAF Fairford, UK, Jeddah Saudi Arabia, Diego Garcia in the Indian Ocean and from the continental United States. Several hours prior to the first tactical air strikes, seven B-52Gs launched from Barksdale AFB, Louisiana, loaded with conventionally armed AGM-86C cruise missiles programed to strike strategic targets deep in Iraq. The flight lasted a total of 35 hours and proved that the old BUFF still possesses global reach.

The largest deployment in the history of the U-2 program took place in August 1990. It involved the movement of U-2Rs and TR-1As from Beale AFB and RAF Alconbury, to the Gulf Theatre of Operations. Reconnaissance flights began early in Operation Desert Shield. Missions were launched from Taif AB, Saudi Arabia and RAF Akrotiri, Cyprus. Flying around-the-clock, U-2Rs and TR-1As were able to provide near real time intelligence and reconnaissance information concerning the movement of Iraqi forces.

B-52G, 57-6501, RAGIN' RED, of the 416th BW, displays black bomb symbols for missions launched from Moron AB., Spain. In addition, it carries white mission markings for sorties flown from Jeddah, Saudi Arabia. (Michael P. Kopack Sr.)

B-52G, 57-6515, MOHAWK VALLEY, of the 416th BW. The name is derived from New York's Mohawk Valley, where the unit is based at Griffis AFB. According to wing public affairs, the camel and palm tree indicate various tactics used on some missions. (Tony Cassanova)

THE WITCH, B-52G, 58-0181, 2nd BW, carries an impressive number and variety of markings. Of historical note is the nose art which originally was carried on B-24D, 41-1840, of the 343rd Bombardment Squadron. That Liberator, crash landed in Yugoslavia on 1 August 1943, following an attack on the Ploesti oil refinery. (Barry Roop)

B-52G, 58-0249, URBAN RENEWAL, of the 379th BW, was another Desert Storm combatant which emerged from the conflict with World War II nose art. This example originally flew on a succession of P-51D's named "Petie", which were assigned to LtCol John C. Meyer, 352nd Fighter Group, 8th Air Force. (Bob Shane)

B-52G, 56-2602, YANKEE DOODLE, 2nd BW, during an air show appearance shortly after the war. Although it carries mission markings, according to this author's research, it did not fly combat missions during Desert Storm. (Douglas Zalud)

This lineup of 416th BW, B-52Gs just back from the Gulf illustrates how far the various bomb wings went to remove all markings. Although some nose art can be seen, the giant Statue of Liberty, which usually adorned these BUFFs, has been completely painted out. The bomber closest to the camera, 57-6498, features a row of red bomb symbols indicating it launched on those missions from RAF Fairford. (Tony Cassanova)

The mission markings on B-52G, 57-0170, SPECIAL DELIVERY II, appear to indicate three missions flown from RAF Fairford (red slash), and seventeen flown from Moron AB., Spain. (John Grech)

B-52G, 59-2580, SHERIFF'S POSSE NO. 2, flew with the 416th BW, from Moron AB., Spain. It is yet another example of World War II nose art. (Andy Thomson)

SPECIAL DELIVERY, B-52G, 58-0204, 379th BW. While assigned to the 806th BW(P), this well executed art work was painted out as were many other examples on BUFFs flying in the Gulf. (Author)

Red bomb symbols applied to EQUIPOISE II, a B-52G, of the 2nd BW, signify sorties flown from RAF Fairford. The two black silhouettes indicate it also flew from Moron AB, Spain. (Barry Roop)

B-52G's of the 93rd BW, flew missions from two locations during Desert Storm. While assigned to the 806th BW(P), they launched from RAF Fairford and from Jeddah Saudi Arabia while part of the 1708th BW(P). Of interest is the large drag chute used to slow the B-52 upon landing. (Michael P. Kopack Jr.)

WHAT'S UP DOC, B-52G, 58-0182, of the 379th BW, photographed prior to the air campaign. During Desert Storm, it flew the majority of its missions from RAF Fairford as part of the 806th BW(Provisional). (Author)

Had it succeeded, the longest combat mission of the war would have been carried out by B-52Gs flying from Wurtsmith AFB, Michigan, to targets in Iraq. Unfortunately, a number of "snafus" resulted in the mission being recalled. Even though no bombs were dropped, the mission still clearly demonstrated the global reach of the B-52. (Brian C. Rogers)

Above: KC-135E, 58-0078, ACES HIGH, of the 150th ARS/170th ARG, New Jersey Air National Guard. (Barry Roop)

The 161st Air Refueling Group, Arizona ANG, flew its Desert Shield missions while assigned to the 1701st ARW(P). This 161st KC-135E, 57-1495, displays nose art and legend "Blackbird We Deliver." During Desert Storm, the unit 'back-filled' for the Kansas ANG and was based at Topeka KS. (Andy Thomson)

HAWG WILD, KC-135E, 56-3638, of the 161st ARG, Arizona ANG. (Bob Shane)

This KC-135E, 58-0116, carries Desert Storm missions near the 161st Group badge. Under the Phoenix, "Desert Storm" appears in very small print. (Bob Shane)

Left: HOT STUFF, KC-135E, 55-3143, of the 161st ARG/197th ARS. Of interest are the stylized Arabic serial number. (Bob Shane)

KC-135R, of the 28th ARS/28th BW, normally based at Ellsworth AFB, SD, but deployed to Muscat-Seeb Oman as part of the 1702nd ARW(Provisional) during Desert Storm. (Rick Morgan)

USAF tankers such as this KC-135R of the 319th ARW, not only refueled USAF, USN and Marine aircraft, they were responsible for refueling several coalition aircraft such as these Canadian Armed Forces CF-18's. (Rick Morgan)

KC-135R, of the 19th ARW equipped with a flying boom which has been modified to permit refueling of USN aircraft such as this F-14 Tomcat. (Rick Morgan)

The glossy paint scheme on this 19th ARW, KC-135R greatly reduced the cabin temperature in comparison with the dark gray tankers. (Rick Morgan)

Although no longer the "Cadillac" of the refueling fleet. Nearly every available KC-135 was pressed into service during Desert Shield/Desert Storm. This red Cadillac appeared on KC-135A, 59-1496 of the 93rd BW. (DOD)

RADCOOL REFUEL, KC-135A, 59-1501, of the 379th BW, depicts a cartoon cheetah from a popular American snack food advertisement. (DOD)

"Saudi Sand Bandit", KC-135R, of the 19th ARW. The nose art has been painted over so not to offend our Saudi hosts. (Author)

KC-135A, 58-0066, SUPERMAN II, 2nd BW. (DOD)

The introduction into service of the KC-10A Extender added a new dimension to rapid deployment. Capable of hauling 170,000-lbs., over a distance of 3,797 nm, a couple of KC-10s can move entire fighter squadrons, fighters, ground equipment and personnel. (Rick Morgan)

The KC-10A is equipped with a flying boom as well as the drogue and hose system. This enables the Extender to refuel USAF, USN and foreign designs without modification. At least one KC-10A has been modified with underwing hose systems which permit refueling three aircraft at once. (Rick Morgan)

KC-10A, 83-0082, BAYOU BABE, 2nd BW. (DOD)

KC-10A, 85-0034, LOUISIANA YARD DOG, 2nd BW. (Author)

RUSHIN NIGHTMARE, B-52G, 59-2583, of the 416th BW, flew thirty-seven combat missions from Jeddah, Saudi Arabia, while assigned to the 1708th BW(P). The five black bomb symbols are indicative of missions launched from Moron AB, Spain. (Tony Cassanova)

B-52G, 58-0159, ALLEY OOP'S BOLD ASSAULT, 379th BW. Normally based at Wurtsmith AFB, Michigan, this BUFF flew twenty-four missions from Jeddah Saudi Arabia. In addition it flew missions from Moron Spain. (Brian C. Rogers)

OLD CROW EXPRESS, B-52G, 57-6492, 379th BW, returning from a mission with empty bomb racks. A "cell" of three B-52's, were capable of dropping one hundred fifty-three, M-117 750-lb bombs. Known as "carpet bombing", the psychological effects were as devastating as the physical damage. One captured Iraqi troop commander stated he surrendered because of the B-52 attacks. Not because his position had been attacked, because he had seen one which had been bombed by B-52s. (Brian C. Rogers)

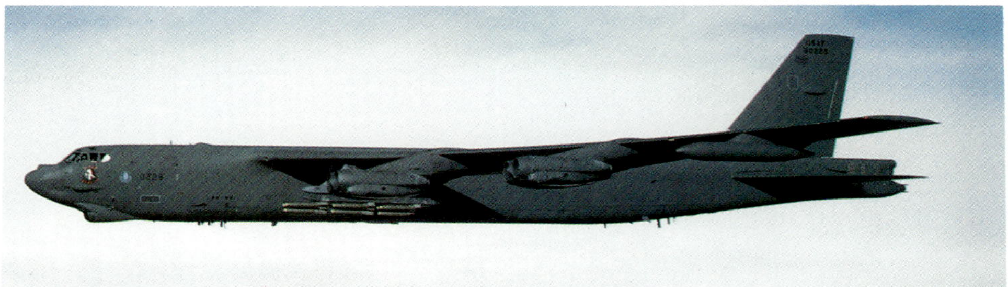

A B-52G of the 93rd BW hauling a full load of MK-82 High Drag bombs. The MK-82 AIR, is equipped with a small chute which deploys to retard the bombs descent. This feature enables the B-52 to deliver 500-lb bombs at low level. (Brian C. Rogers)

KC-135E, 58-0085, CALIFORNIA DREAMIN, 336th ARS, AFres, based at March AFB, CA. Nose art appears to be a killer whale, possibly, "Shamu." The dark gray over Boeing light gray paint scheme is often referred to as the "Shamu" scheme. (Keith Snyder)

Mission markings on CALIFORNIA DREAMIN consist of Desert Shield markings in yellow and Desert Storm in red. (Keith Snyder)

Right: KC-135E, 59-1505, 133rd ARS, New Hampshire ANG. The white markings represent Desert Storm missions, the yellow ribbons represent ferry flights home. (Peter Wilson) Below: Full side view of KC-135E, 59-1505, 133rd ARS. (Jim Tunney)

Above: KC-135E, 108th ARS/126th ARW, Illinois ANG, preparing to refuel an F-14 Tomcat. (Rick Morgan)

KC-135E, 57-1448, ARTIC TRAVELER, 168th ARS, carries a variety of markings. The large black camel and small red camel represent Desert Storm missions. The remaining markings are from Desert Shield. The nose art was applied following its return from the Gulf. Of interest are the last four digits of the serial number which has been repeated in Arabic. (Author)

KC-135A, 62-3498, ARKANSAS EAGLE, of the 97th ARS/97th BW, Eaker AFB, AR. During the air campaign it flew from Jeddah, Saudi Arabia as part of the 1709th ARW(P). (DOD)

KC-135E, 57-1512, KUKAI MARU, 336th ARS/ 452nd ARW, AFres. (Andy Thomson)

Left: KC-135, 58-0005, OL LIGHTNEN of the 117th ARS/190th ARG, Kansas ANG.

Above: Normally based at Grissom AFB, Indiana, KC-135E, 59-1477, of the 72nd ARS/ 434th ARW, AFres, flew the majority of its Desert Storm missions from King Abdul Aziz IAP, Saudi Arabia. (Jeff Rankin-Lowe/Sirius)

Mission markings on KC-135E, 59-1493, of the 132nd ARS 101st ARW, Maine ANG. (Mike Reyno)

Glossy gray KC-135E, of the 145th ARS/160th ARG, Ohio ANG. (Rick Morgan)

Left and below: KC-10A, 86-0036, PEACE MAKER, of the 68th ARW, returns to Seymour Johnson AFB, following its deployment to the Gulf during Desert Shield/Desert Storm. (Author)

Left: KC-10A Extenders not only deliver fuel but they receive it as well. Referred to as "swapping spit", MYSTIC WARRIOR, 86-0031, of the 68th ARW, receives a couple hundred pounds of fuel from another KC-10A. (Author)

Right and below: KC-10A, 79-1950, CITY OF MORENO VALLEY, from the 22nd ARW, departs on another refueling mission. Desert Storm markings on 22nd ARW KC-10s consisted of black clouds and lightning bolts. (Author)

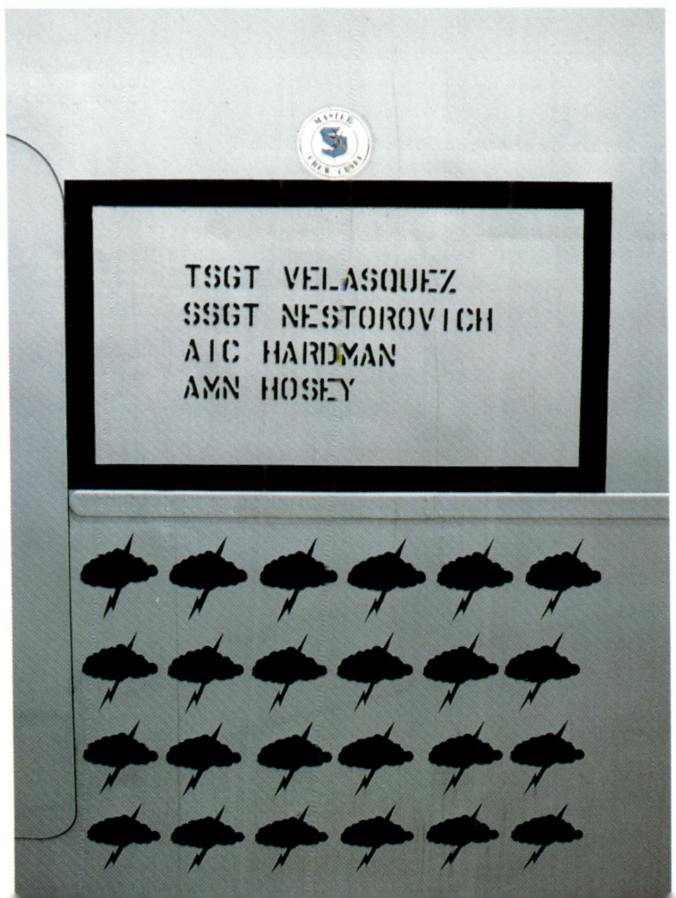

KC-10A Extender of the 1709th ARW(Provisional) refuels a flight of F-16C Falcons on an early morning mission. During Desert Shield/Desert Storm, the USAF discovered the Navy's probe and drogue method permitted the refueling of more aircraft in less time than the flying boom method currently employed. (Rick Morgan)

GHOST RIDER, A KC-10A Extender of the 68th ARW. Nose art on all 68th ARW KC-10s was very well executed and quite appealing. (Author)

KC-10A, 85-0030, WAR LORD, 68th ARW. (Author)

KC-10A, 86-0030, LUCKY LISA, 68th ARW. (Author)

KC-10A, 87-0124, SPIRIT OF KITTY HAWK, is the flagship of the 68th ARW and the last KC-10A to roll off the assembly line. (Author)

KC-10A, 84-0189, ACE OF SPADES, 68th ARW. (Author)

KC-10A, 86-0029, BLACK KNIGHT, 68th ARW. (Author)

KC-10A, 83-0077, GREAT WHITE, an appropriate name for this gloss white and Douglas gray Extender of the 68th ARW. (Author)

KC-135Q, 58-0054, BAD BART from the 349th ARS/9th SRW. American cartoon character "Bart Simpson" went to war during Desert Storm on more aircraft than all other cartoon characters combined. On this Stratotanker a new twist has been added to his infamous "Eat My Shorts" slogan. (Brian C. Rogers)

The current KC-10A, scheme, consisting of Gunship gray over Douglas gray is giving way to a monochromatic scheme of a lighter shade of gray. In the gulf, the desert sun often overheated the cabins of the dark gray Extenders. (Author)

KC-135Q, 58-0112, of the 9th SRW, displays a Stegosaurus with KC-135 wing and an SR-71 which bears a striking resemblance to a Pterandon. The artwork appears to be a parody concerning the types length of service. Of interest are the toned down Arabic numerals. (DOD)

View of a KC-10A Extender as seen from a number of Coalition aircraft during Desert Shield/Desert Storm. KC-10s were responsible for saving at least one aircraft, an F-111F when the Aardvarks base was fogged in and it nearly ran out of fuel. (Author)

A KC-135E, of the 171st ARW, Pennsylvania Air National Guard refuels F-14 Tomcats from three different squadrons, VF-84, VF-41 and VF-102. (Rick Morgan)

The 9th SRW was not the only unit to deploy the KC-135Q to the Gulf region. This example is from the 380th ARS normally based at Plattsburgh AFB, New York. (Kevin Foy)

The KC-135R is not the designation selected for a reconnaissance version of this tanker. Instead it denotes those KC-135's which have been re-engined with F-108-CF-100 (CFM-56) powerplants. The modification not only changed the KC-135s outward appearance, it greatly improved its performance permitting shorter takeoffs, without the need for water injection. At least eleven KC-135R units deployed to the Gulf. This example, 57-1469, CENTURION, is from the 42nd BW. The nose art was applied after the Gulf war. (Author)

KC-135Q, 59-1504, of the 9th SRW, displays the Christmas spirit during Operation Desert Shield. (DOD)

Mission markings were applied to all KC-135R's from the 42nd BW, which took part in Operation Desert Shield/Desert Storm. This example was typical of those markings. (Author)

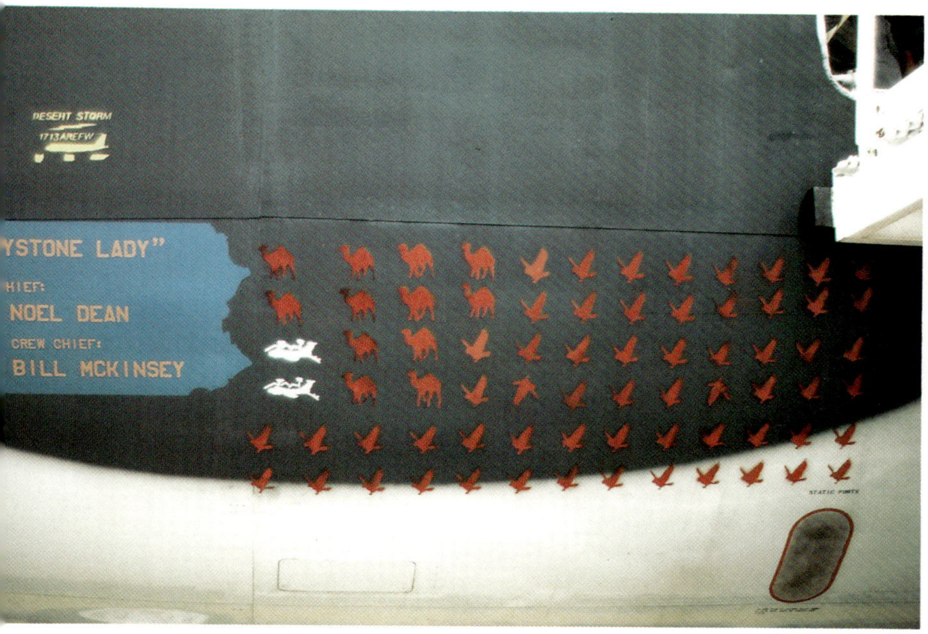

KC-135E, 57-2595, KEYSTONE LADY, of the 147th ARS/171st ARW, Pennsylvania ANG, displays a variety of mission markings. The red camels represent missions flown from Saudi Arabia while the red hawks are missions flown from Dubai IAP, in the Unite Arab Emirates. The white KC-135 silhouettes indicate ferry flights home. Of interest is the 1713th AREFW stencil above the state of Pennsylvania. (Author)

FUELIN' AROUND on KC-135E, 57-2608, from the 147th ARS, Pennsylvania Air National Guard. (MSGT. William L. Gall)

Below: KC-135E, 56-3643, HIGH OCTANE TAZ, of the 151st ARS/134th ARG, Tennesse ANG. (DOD)

While the Tactical Air Command was busy removing Gulf war nose art and mission markings, SAC units, such as the 42nd Bomb Wing, were busy reapplying it. B-52G, 58-0257, FIRST STRIKE, with neatly painted bomb symbols brings to mind the nose art and mission markings applied to the World War II bomber fleet. (Tony Cassanova)

42nd BW, B-52G rests on the ramp at Diego Garcia. The BUFF is loaded with M-117, 750-lb bombs. Dropping these from 35-40,000 feet, Iraqi troops would not become aware they were under attack until the bombs started to explode among their positions. (Brian C. Rogers)

B-52G of the 42nd BW, returning from a mission. Note the empty underwing racks which are capable of accommodating 9 bombs each. An additional 27 can be carried internally. (Brian C. Rogers)

Left: EAST COAST OUTLAW, B-52G, 58-0192, of the 42nd BW, is a fine example of SAC nose art applied after Desert Storm. (Author)

Above: B-52G, 58-0195, ETERNAL GUARDIAN, displays forty-six bomb symbols and the 42nd BW badge. The 42nd can trace its history to the 42nd Bombardment Group which saw combat in the Pacific during World War II. (Author)

Left: A 42nd BW, B-52G refuels from a KC-10A over the Persian Gulf. The BUFF is enroute to targets in the KTO loaded with 51 M-117, 750-lb bombs. (Dennis Smith)

E-3B/C Sentry aircraft of the 552nd AW & CW flew missions from Riyadh Military City Airport and from Incirlik, Turkey. From early in Desert Shield, an E-3, or AWACs as it is commonly referred, was constantly airborne providing control of coalition air assets and monitoring any Iraqi threats which might materialize. (DOD)

The EC-130E was operated in the Gulf by the 7th ACCS as an airborne command and control center. The type was capable of pinpointing Iraqi targets such as armor columns. Of interest is the row of camels above the crew entrance. (Kevin Foy)

RC-135V of the 55th SRW, departs on another intelligence gathering mission. These aircraft were some of the first USAF types to arrive in the Gulf. By the eve of Desert Storm, an RC-135 was airborne twenty-four hours a day gathering valuable intelligence data concerning the Iraqi threat. (Via author)

Its time aloft limited only by crew endurance, this Compass Call EC-130H of the 41st ECS, approaches a KC-135 for additional fuel. The EC-130H created havoc with Iraqi communications during Desert Storm. (Sergio Bottaro)

UNITED STATES NAVY

At the time of the invasion, the United States Navy and the Marine Corps Joint Task Forces Southwest Asia were immediately placed on a heightened stated of readiness. Two aircraft carries in the region, the USS Independence/CV-62, and the USS Dwight D. Eisenhower/CVN-69, were ordered to the Gulf of Oman and the Red Sea. Upon arrival, these two carrier battle groups constituted the first US military assets capable of projecting power to the heartland of Iraq. Joining and later relieving the USS Independence and USS Eisenhower were six additional carriers: USS America/CV-66, USS Ranger/CV-61, USS John F. Kennedy/CV-67, USS Midway/CV-41, USS Theodore Roosevelt/CVn-71 and the USS Saratoga/CV-60.

By the eve of Operation Desert Storm, six carriers were in position to launch strikes in support of the air campaign. When preparations got underway for an assault on Iraqi forces in Kuwait, the USS America moved from the Red Sea to the Persian Gulf, where it joined the USS Ranger and USS Midway. Late in the war the USS Theodore Roosevelt also entered the Persian Gulf conducting operations there through Desert Storm and Operation Provide Comfort.

There were six Carrier Air Wings deployed to the Gulf region during Operation Desert Shield/Desert Storm. Each wing consisted of a variety of aircraft. F-14A/B Tomcats or F/A-18A/C Hornets were assigned to defend the strike package, provide CAP or as was the case with the Hornet, deliver ordnance. Each air wing was assigned at least one squadron of A-6E Intruders utilized in the all weather, long range medium attack role. Light attack was assumed by F/A-18 Hornets and A-7E Corsairs. The latter was making its final combat cruise prior to retirement from USN service. Each carrier was equipped with long range surveillance aircraft the E-2C Hawkeye. The EA-6B Prowler accompanied the strike package providing additional security by jamming Iraqi radar. Normally, the S-3A/B Viking, would be assigned the Anti-Submarine role but due to the lack of an Iraqi submarine threat, the Vikings were tasked with targeting and attacking surface ships and land based radar sites. In-flight refueling was provided by tanker versions of the Intruder, the KA-6D. Supplementing these Intruders were S-3s, A-6Es and even F/A-18s equipped with a buddy pack refueling store. The USN was tasked with some of the longest missions of the war. Strike packages therefore had to rely on USAF and ANG tankers for gas to and from the target area. Finally, rotary wing aircraft assigned to the air wings consisted of the SH-3H Sea King helicopter. Normally assigned to ASW, they were pressed into service providing strike rescue, logistical support and mine countermeasures.

In addition to those aircraft assigned to carrier air wings, a variety of USN types played a key role in the air war. These included the EA-3B Skywarriors which flew their final combat sorties of a long career. (The Skywarrior was retired from active service along with the Corsair II within weeks of returning from the Gulf). A number of P-3 Orion squadrons were also present and played an active if not overlooked role in the air campaign. Several logistical support aircraft played a critical role supplying crucial parts and delivering tons of mail. These seldom mentioned types consisted of C-9Bs, UC-12Bs, C-2A Greyhounds and US-3A Vikings.

Aboard the USS Ranger, H-hour on 17 January arrived with the playing of the "William Tell Overture" from every loudspeaker aboard ship. It signaled the first combat air strikes launched from the deck of the Ranger since the Vietnam war. The target was Umm Qsar Naval Base. During the opening phase of the Gulf war, the Persian Gulf carrier air wings were tasked with the destruction of the Iraqi navy. This mission was accomplished with a variety of ordnance including Harpoon and Skipper missiles as well as Rockeye cluster bombs, Iron bombs, and even a D-704 refueling pod. Over-the-horizon targeting was provided by P-3C Orions equipped with a newly developed system 'Outlaw Hunter.' As a result, a total of forty-eight Iraqi ships of various types were destroyed or disabled by the USN.

Meanwhile, in the Red Sea, air strikes were being launched against a number of targets deep in Iraq. These included suppression of enemy air defenses (SEAD), command and control centers and airfields. As the ground war commenced the emphasis was switched to armor, artillery, transport and bridges. In all, naval aviators contributed 20,000 combat sorties to the 112,000 flown by Coalition aircraft.

While flying strike escort missions, F-14 Tomcats were usually configured with the AIM-54C Phoenix, AIM-7F/M Sparrow and AIM-9L/M Sidewinder. (LCdr. Art Legare USN)

F-14A, Tomcat, 162704, of VF-102, displays a high visibility paint scheme. The markings of VF-102, the Diamondbacks, have changed little in the past ten years. (Author)

Markings such as CHRISTINE, on F-14A, 160399, of VF-33, were scarce on USN aircraft. The "AB" tailcode indicates this Tomcat was assigned to CVW-1, based at NAS Oceana. During Desert Storm, VF-33 flew CAP and MiG sweep missions for every air wing strike launched from the Red Sea. (Mike Grove)

Jubilant A-6E crew of VA-85 proudly display the stars and bars while approaching a welcome home celebration at NAS Oceana on 17 April, 1991. VA-85 dropped more than 750 tons of ordnance during Desert Storm. Of interest are the mission symbols below the Bombardier Navigator. (Author)

The KA-6D, aerial refueling version of the A-6 Intruder, played a key role in supporting strike packages. Note the high visibility paint scheme designed to make it stand out from attack variants of the Intruder. (Author)

The F/A-18C has become the primary replacement for the A-7E Corsair II in US Navy light attack squadrons. This particular Hornet of VFA-86, (Sidewinders) returned from the Gulf with impressive mission markings consisting of general purpose bombs, HARMs and a Walleye. (Jeff Puzzullo)

The E-2C Hawkeye routinely flew some of the longest missions of the Gulf war often penetrating Iraqi airspace in order to provide AEW on deep penetration missions. (Mike Grove)

Close up of Intruder which displays mission markings typical of returning VA-85, A-6E's. (Author)

Commanders S-3A, Viking of VS-22. The majority of U.S. Navy aircraft participating in the Gulf War were painted in low visibility schemes similar to this S-3A. (Author)

As evidenced by the mission markings, bombs and lightning bolts, this E-2C, of VAW-123, escorted four bombing strikes providing AEW. (John Grech)

Nose art on USN aircraft was extremely scarce. This buxom Beauty adorned a S-3B Viking of "The World Famous Maulers" of VS-32. (Author)

Left: On 20 February, 1991, while on an armed surface reconnaissance mission, the USS Valley Forge (CG-50), vectored VS-32, S-3B, 159765, to investigate an unknown contact near Faylaka Island in the north Persian Gulf. Using ISAR and FLIR, the S-3 identified the target as a hostile ZHUK class gunboat. The Viking initiated an attack but in their zeal to achieve the first ever S-3 surface kill, the crew inadvertently armed both wing stations, one contained three general purpose bombs while the other a D-704 refueling store. Subsequently, the bombs and . . . unconventional ordnance were dropped on the gunboat, resulting in its destruction. Hence the unusual markings which appear on this VS-32 S-3B. (Author)

Above: Tomcats from VF-1, are some of the most colorful in the fleet. Somehow they have managed to forestall the move to low visibility paint schemes. The 100 side number and rainbow tail markings denote this Tomcat as the commander's, or CAG's aircraft. (Author)

Above: On 6 February, 1991, a "Wolf Pack" Tomcat, 162603, downed an Iraqi Mi-8 helicopter with an AIM-9M Sidewinder. Three Iraqi aircraft were downed by USN aircraft during the Gulf war. (Jeff Puzzullo)

Right: The USN and other services have gone to great lengths to reduce the visibility of their aircraft via toned down paint schemes. Compare this low visibility scheme to the VF-1 Commander's Tomcat. (Mike Anselmo)

Without a significant ASW threat, the S-3 Viking, was assigned missions far removed from its traditional one. The Red Griffins of VS-38 took part in the first delivery of the Tactical Air-Launched Decoy (TALD). They also pinpointed Iraqi surface ships with their sophisticated ISAR and FLIR systems. Mission markings on this Viking appear below the aircraft number. (Mike Anselmo)

Above and left: The "Bounty Hunters" of VF-2 deployed both the high and low visibility schemes to the Gulf. The "NE" tailcode signifies assignment to CVW-2 shore based at NAS Miramar, CA. (Mike Anselmo - both)

Close up of VAW-116, markings indicating that this E-2C flew 269 combat hours and 65 combat sorties. (Jeff Puzzullo)

At a distance, it would appear this E-2C of VAW-116 had been credited with an aerial victory. Closer inspection reveals a tally of combat hours and combat sorties painted under the Iraqi flag. The "Sun Kings" of VAW-116, introduced the APS-138 Advanced Processing Radar system to combat during Desert Storm. (Mike Grove)

CVW-2 was unique in possessing two A-6E squadrons. The only carrier to share that distinction in the Gulf was the USS Midway. During the first hours of the air campaign, this massive array of firepower was utilized to attack the Qsar Naval Base at Bubiyan Island in the Persian Gulf. During that attack, an A-6E, from VA-145 made the first Intruder HARM launch under combat conditions. Of interest are the number and variety of mission markings on this VA-145, A-6E. Tail markings appear on top left of opposite page. (Mike Grove)

Below: A total of 49 bomb symbols and one bridge have been applied just below the wing root of this VA-145 Intruder, 162200. The bridge silhouette denotes the destruction of the Shuyukh bridge over the Euphrates River on 27 February 1991. The bridge was destroyed with a pair of 2000-lb LGBs closing the last escape route for the remnants of the Iraqi army fleeing Kuwait. (Mike Anselmo)

Below: VA-145 Intruders destroyed 41 Iraqi naval vessels, plus an unconfirmed number of tanks, trucks, artillery and radar sites. This occurred in just 43 days of combat operations involving 681 sorties. (Michael Anselmo)

Tail markings on VA-155, A-6E. (Mike Grove)

Below: Kill markings on this EA-6B Prowler of VAQ-131, consist of a radar dish in the cross hair of a HARM missile. During the air campaign, the VAQ-131 Lancers, launched twenty-four HARMS. A typical mission involved suppressing Iraqi SAM sites with AGM-88, High Speed Anti-Radiation Missiles designed to home in on the last recorded coordinates of a transmitting radar. Early in the air war at least one HARM was launched per mission. (Mike Anselmo - sideview) (Mike Grove - close up)

The four underwing fuel tanks and centerline refueling pod indicate that this VA-75, A-6E, is pulling double duty as an aerial refueling platform. S-3 Vikings, A-7E Corsair IIs and even F/A-18 Hornets shared the air-to-air refueling chores during Desert Storm. (DOD)

Right and below: These photos show a comparison of mission markings used early and late in the air campaign. VA-75 Intruder, 503, carries the early version consisting of bomb silhouettes aft of the cockpit. Intruder 501 displays the final version, on the nose. (SRA Chris Putman) (Author - 501)

Spotting a tanker quickly can be crucial for a pilot of a fuel starved Hornet or Tomcat. Since the KA-6D and A-6E so greatly resemble each other in the air, the KA-6D, tanker version of the Intruder has retained the high visibility paint scheme of gull gray over gloss white. (Author)

An EA-6B, Prowler of VAQ-130, configured with two AN/ALQ-99 jamming pods, one external fuel tank and one AGM-88 HARM. The capability to launch HARMS was added to the EA-6B with BuNo. 162225. (Jim Tunney)

Desert Shield/Desert Storm, marked the final cruise for the A-7E Corsair II and Attack Squadron 72. Within weeks of returning to NAS Cecil Field, FL, the squadron was disestablished and the A-7E was relegated to museums and AMARC. (Cdr. John Leenhouts USN)

This row of aircraft silhouettes on a KA-6D of VA-75 are not kill markings, they represent 'saves' of fuel starved F-14 Tomcats and F/A-18 Hornets. (Author)

Mission markings typical of VAQ-130 Prowlers. (Author)

Excellent air-to-air study of VA-72's Desert Storm Corsair II. (Cdr. John Leenhouts USN)

Above and right: This particular VA-72, A-7E flew a number of combat missions during Desert Storm, but not wearing this paint scheme. It was applied following the war while aboard the USS John F. Kennedy while returning to the United States. (Author)

Call sign Decoy 403, A-7E, 159999, of VA-72, was the only A-7E Corsair II lost during the war. It was severly damaged during a launch from the USS John F. Kennedy. Decoy 403 was able to make a successful barricade arrestment back aboard the JFK. Following inspection, it was deemed damaged beyond economical repair. All salvageable parts were removed and 403 was pushed over the side. (Cdr. John Leenhouts USN)

Left: An impressive scoreboard of mission markings appeared on this VA-46 Corsair II. Depicted here are symbols indicating delivery of Walleyes, Rockeye cluster bombs, general purpose bombs and anti-radiation missiles. (Author)

A trio of VA-72 Corsair II's return from a mission. Of interest is 402, which retains an AGM-88 HARM on its outboard wing station. During the Gulf war, USN aircraft launched HARMs from EA-6B's, A-6E's, A-7E's and F/A-18's. (Cdr. John Leenhouts USN)

USAF and ANG tankers played a pivotal role during the Gulf war. Here a KC-135E of the 1709th ARW(Provisional) refuels an F-14A of VF-14. The flying boom reads "Kansas Coyotes", indicating this tanker belongs to the 190th ARG/117th ARS, based at Forbes Field, KS. (PH3 Chester O. Falkenhainer USN)

The mission markings on this VA-72 Corsair II indicate that it flew 24 combat sorties, dropped 64 general purpose bombs, 105 cluster bombs, 3 Walleye glide bombs and launched 10 HARMs. (Author)

An A-7E of VA-46 prepares to taxi to the catapult with a light load (for the Corsair II), consisting of eight MK-83, 1000-lb, general purpose bombs and two AIM-9 Sidewinders. (LCdr. Dave Parsons USN)

A KC-135A refuels an EA-6B Prowler of VAQ-130 as a second Prowler and a VF-32, Tomcat await their turn. The tanker seen here has been modified with a hose and drogue to permit refueling of USN and USMC aircraft. (DOD)

Side number 306, indicates this A-7E is assigned to VA-46, one of two Corsair II units making the types final cruise during Operation Desert Storm. (SRA Chris Putman)

As was the case with many aircraft which participated in Desert Storm, this A-7E of VA-46 went to AMARC at Davis Monthan AFB, to await an uncertain fate. (Bob Shane)

A F-14A Tomcat from VF-32, patrols Saudi Arabian airspace. All Tomcats participating in Desert Storm were equipped with a digital data link system, the AN/ASW-27C. The system permitted the Tomcat strike leader to keep track of all Tomcats in the strike package without the benefit of a command and control aircraft such as the Hawkeye or Sentry. The system also transmitted target information to all other AN/ASW-27C equipped aircraft. (DOD)

An interesting two-tone mottled effect has been applied to this VF-14 Tomcat. The colorful markings on the vertical stabilizer combined with the double nuts (00) on the rudder, indicate this Tomcat is assigned to the commanding officer of VF-14. (Author)

Right: Tomcat squadrons maintain at least one F-14 in high visibility markings. Although attractive and eye-catching on the air show circuit, these markings could prove fatal in combat because of their high visibility. These 'show birds' were toned-down with a coat of flat gray water soluble paint prior to flying combat sorties. (Author)

Below: An F-14A, Radar Intercept Officers view as his Tomcat refuels from a KC-135R. (DOD)

Special 'Desert Storm' markings applied to the VF-32 commander's F-14A Tomcat. (Author)

During Desert Storm, the Grumman E-2C performed a number of important missions including strike control, SAR and AEW. Hawkeyes of VAW-126 flew a total of 176 combat missions during the war. (Author)

Fourteen lightning bolt mission markings appear as on the side of the VAW-126 commander's E-2C. (Author)

The S-3B made its combat debut during Desert Storm. Employing ISAR and FLIR, the Vikings were successful in identifying and targeting a number of radar sites and Scud launchers as evidenced by mission markings applied to this VS-22, S-3B. (Author)

An S-3B of VS-22 employs a D-704 buddy refueling store to refuel another Navy aircraft. (DOD)

This SH-3H, of HS-7 displays a ship silhouette. It is not a kill marking; it represents an escort mission involving an armed inspection of a vessel during the blockade of Iraq. (PH3 Paul A. Hawthorne)

Although VA-185 possessed the KA-6D tanker version of the Intruder, the need for aerial refueling was so great that A-6E's were routinely configured as tankers via the addition of refueling pods and extra external fuel tanks. (Mike Anselmo)

Busy pre-strike flight deck as "ordies" or "red shirts" move cluster bombs and general purpose bombs in preparation for another strike. (USN)

Pre-war photograph of a F/A-18A of VFA-151 which was assigned to CVW-5 during the Gulf war. CVW-5 was embarked aboard the USS Midway (CV-41) and operated in the Persian Gulf during the war. (Mike Grove)

The "Golden Dragons" of VFA-192 flew strike missions deep into Iraq delivering a variety of ordnance including cluster bombs, general purpose bombs and HARM missiles. The multi-role capability of the Hornet allowed it to serve as the Midway's light attack and strike defense assets. (Mike Grove)

During the air campaign, the majority of precision guided ordnance was delivered by the USAF. However, A-6E squadrons such as VA-115 and VA-185 launched a number of "smart bombs", as evidenced by these mission markings. (Mike Anselmo)

An F-14A Tomcat of VF-41, the "Black Aces" participates in a CAP mission somewhere over the Persian Gulf, armed with AIM-9 Sidewinder and AIM-7 Sparrow air-to-air missiles. (Lt. Gerald B. Parsons USN)

The patchwork of grays on this VF-84 Tomcat are the result of attempts at corrosion control. Constant exposure to salt air plays havoc with the paint schemes of USN aircraft. (Lt. Gerald B. Parsons USN)

In addition to its primary mission of fleet air defense, Tomcats, such as this example from VF-84, flew combat air patrol (TARCAP), barrier air patrol (BARCAP) and MiG sweeps. F-14 also flew HUVCAP missions to protect high value assets such as E-3 Sentrys. (Rick Morgan)

Plane captain of VFA-15 prepares his Hornet for a sortie. This F/A-18A is loaded with MK-82 500-lb bombs. Mounted on the left Sparrow station is a laser Spot Tracker (LST) pod. (Rick Morgan)

Special tail markings and a high visibility paint scheme indicate this VF-84 Tomcat is assigned to the squadron commander. (Author)

Two Hornet squadrons, VFA-15 and 87, made up the light attack complement aboard the USS Theodore Roosevelt. This example, from VFA-87 was photographed shortly after the war during a Canadian port-of-call. (Mike Reyno)

Although this VA-65 Intruder is loaded with MK-82 low drag bombs, the A-6E is quite capable of delivering an array of ordnance which includes the Paveway I and II, Shrike, Walleye, Skipper II, SLAM, Harpoon, HARM and air launched decoys. (Rick Morgan)

"Hose Multiplying" was an aerial refueling technique involving a KA-6D and a KC-10A or KC-135 modified with hose and drogue. In this case, an A-6E with buddy store refueling pod refuels an F/A-18A from VFA-87. The A-6E would refill its tanks from the tanker and continue to refuel strike aircraft. This method permitted more aircraft to refuel in less time utilizing a single tanker. (Rick Morgan)

Right: This A-6E of VA-65, carries only Rockeye cluster bombs and GBU-16s. During the final hours of the air campaign, aircraft attacked the Iraqi Army as it fled north from Kuwait. This engagement became known to some as the I-5 shootout. During this engagement USN aircraft were being turned around so rapidly, they often launched without full loads of ordnance, loaded with whatever was readily available on deck. (Rick Morgan)

Below: A pair of VA-65 Intruders received a new desert paint job during Desert Storm. This experimental scheme was not adopted throughout the wing as it proved too effective, as other VA-65 pilots would lose sight of these Intruders while overflying the desert. (Rick Morgan)

Below: Tail markings carried on the rudders of VA-65 Intruders. The squadron is known as the "Tigers." (Author)

Tail markings on one of two Intruders painted in a special water soluble desert scheme. (Rick Morgan)

The "Roadrunners" of VA-36 served alongside VA-65 aboard the USS Theodore Roosevelt during Desert Shield and Desert Storm. Shortly after returning to NAS Oceana the unit was disestablished. (Author)

This Intruder from VA-65 has its tailhook lowered as if preparing to land aboard a carrier. Of interest is the buddy pack refueling pod and three external fuel tanks. (Rick Morgan)

EVE OF DESTRUCTION, EA-6B, 163527, of VAQ-141. This squadron flew one of the deepest penetrations of Iraqi airspace made by USN aircraft when it escorted an RAF strike 180 miles into Iraq. (LCdr. Rick Morgan USN)

The "Scouts" of VS-24, was the first S-3B Viking unit to conduct overland strikes attacking AAA and Silkworm sites. (DOD)

Right: Mission markings in the form of bomb silhouettes indicate this VA-36 Intruder flew 60 combat sorties during the Gulf war. (Author)

Formation flyby of VAW-124, E-2C Hawkeyes upon the squadrons return to NAS Norfolk, 26 June 1991. (Author)

Without an ASW threat, Sea Kings, such as this example from HS-9, flew an increased pace of plane guard, carrier-on-board delivery and anti-mine missions. (Rick Morgan)

Carrier Air Wing Eight was the only wing to encourage the application of nose art. One aircraft from each squadron was selected to have nose art applied. Whether applied by hand or airbrush, what emerged was the finest artwork viewed on any USN aircraft returning from the Gulf war. Unfortunately few examples survived long enough to reach the US and stateside viewing. (Rick Morgan)

HEARTLESS, A-6E, VA-36. (Rick Morgan

EVE OF DESTRUCTION, EA-6B, 163527, VAQ-141. (Rick Morgan)

Right: EYE'S OF THE STORM, S-3B, VS-24. (Rick Morgan)

One of the finest examples of nose art to emerge from the Gulf, was MISS B HAVIN, on E-2C, 161552, of VAW-124. When this Hawkeye was photographed upon its return to NAS Norfolk, it displayed no visible nose art. All nose art was ordered removed prior to each squadron launching from the USS Theodore Roosevelt for the return flight home. Apparently, an enterprising sailor decided to preserve MISS B HAVIN under a protective layer of paper, which was oversprayed with gray paint and gave the appearance of being painted out. At Norfolk, the protection was carefully peeled away revealing this work of art. (Author)

Below: CLASSIC, E-2C, 161552, VAW-124. This example of nose art was later changed to MISS B HAVIN. (Rick Morgan)

"Garfield", A-6E, VA-65. (Rick Morgan)

Left: QUEEN OF SPADES, F-14A, 162689, VF-41. (Rick Morgan)

CAT SNATCH FEVER, F-14A, 162692, VF-84. (Rick Morgan)

Carrier Air Wing Seventeen was the only air wing to deploy the F-14B during Desert Storm. Previously designated F-14A(Plus), the F-14B incorporates more powerful engines, the F100-GE-400. This view of a VF-74, F-14B, reveals the primary external difference, enlarged and redesigned engine nozzles. (Author)

The "Sluggers" of VF-103 also deployed the F-14B as part of CVW-17. The squadron was one of the first to reequip with the type. VF-103 experienced the only Tomcat loss of the war when 161430, callsign CLUBLEAF 212, was downed during a mission on 21 January 1991. The pilot, Lt. Devon Jones was rescued by USAF Special Operations helicopter. His RIO, Lt. Lawrence Slade was taken prisoner. (Author)

During the Gulf war two F/A-18C Hornet squadrons, VFA-81 and 83 were assigned to CVW-17, aboard the USS Saratoga. This particular Hornet is easily recognizable as the commander's aircraft due to its abundance of colorful markings which feature the CVW-17 badge on the vertical stabalizer. The paint scheme was dedicated to a squadronmate killed in a pre-war accident. (Author)

Right: During the air campaign, the USN recorded only two aerial victories against fixed wing Iraqi aircraft. Both kills were registered by F/A-18C's, of VFA-81, on 17 January 1991. This F/A-18C, 163502, was flown by Lt. Frank Mongillo who engaged a pair of MiG-21s with his wingman LCdr. Mark Fox. Lt. Mongillo downed one MiG with a single AIM-7 Sparrow while the wingman got the second with an AIM-7 and AIM-9 (below). (Mike Grove)

Right and below: The MiG kills scored by Lt. Mongillo and LCdr. Fox may not have been achieved were it not for an E-2C, of VAW-125, which was providing air control, monitoring the airborne threats, it alerted the Hornets of the presence of MiGs. Two MiG-21 silhouettes were applied to the commander's Hawkeye following the engagement. (Author)

An A-6E, from VA-35, callsign RAYGUN 511, photographed enroute to a target in Iraq. This Intruder is armed with GBU-16's (2000-lb, Paveway II LGBs). An Intruder from VA-35 was responsible for the destruction of an Iraqi bridge just after a motorist, ("the luckiest man in Iraq"), had crossed it. (LCdr. Brian Scott USN)

The importance of aerial refueling cannot be overstated in relation to its effect on the overall triumph of airpower during the Gulf war. This unidentified KC-135 utilizes a hose and drogue to refuel an Intruder from VA-35. (LCdr. Brian Scott USN)

Lt. Jeff Zaun became a POW on the first night of the war when his A-6E, 161668, was downed while conducting a night attack against a heavily defended airfield in western Iraq. This Intruder, which bears his name, was an attrition replacement, drawn from the eastcoast A-6E training squadron, VA-42. (Author)

Several Intruders flying combat in Desert Storm also flew combat during the Vietnam war. A-6E, 155661, of VA-35 is one such Intruder having flown a number of Vietnam combat sorties from the deck of the USS Coral Sea (CV-43) while serving with VMA(AW)-224, a USMC squadron. (Author)

Generally, USN Intruder squadrons have four KA-6D's assigned for the aerial refueling mission. This example, returning to NAS Oceana on 27 March 1991, is also equipped with a buddy store refueling pod in addition to its own internal drogue and hose. (Author)

Right and below: Prowlers played an active role in suppressing Iraqi air defenses. Sixty percent of all such missions were flown by USN aircraft. Mission markings applied to this EA-6B of VAQ-132, consisted of red HARMs zeroing in on a radar dish. (Mike Grove)

Right and below: This VS-30 Viking named the WAR HOOVER participated in 44 strike support missions, 38 SUCAP missions (armed with cluster bombs), in addition to tanker and logistical support missions. "Hoover" is the name given to the S-3 because of the sound its engines make. (Barry Roop)

Below: SH-3H of HS-3, displays two ship silhouettes below the pilot's window. These are mission markings for escorting boarding parties during the naval blockade of Iraq. (Rick Morgan)

A catapult officer gives the signal to launch an aircraft from the deck of the USS Saratoga (CV-60). Although these men often performed their mission away from the limelight created by television news cameras, and therefore was less heralded than their shore-based brethern, their contribution to victory was no less significant. (Chris Putman)

MISCELLANEOUS ROTARY/FIXED WING NAVAL AIRCRAFT

Four fleet Sea Knight squadrons were deployed to support Desert Shield/Desert Storm USN logistical operations. This example is from HC-5, Det-4 based aboard the USS Kilauea. Of interest is the Club BOHICA name. "BOHICA" is an abbreviation for "Bend Over Here It Comes Again." (Rick Morgan)

HC-11, Det-3, Sea Knight delivers supplies to the USS Theodore Roosevelt. This HH-46A flew from the USS Shasta during the Gulf war. (Rick Morgan)

Below: Sea Kings such as this example from HC-2, Det-2 kept tons of mail moving to the carriers in the Red Sea and Persian Gulf. (Rick Morgan)

HEROES ON A CLAMSHELL, HC-5 Sea Knight photographed during Desert Shield. (DOD)

A number of HSL, or Helicopter Anti-Submarine squadrons deployed to the Gulf. Normally operated from seaborne platforms, SH-60Bs such as this one from HSL-42, conducted mine spotting and SAR operations. On 24 January, 1991, a HS-60B, Seahawk from HSL 44 rescued an F-16 pilot who parachuted into the Persian Gulf after his Falcon had been hit during a mission over Iraq. (Kevin Foy)

Two MH-53E Sea Dragon squadrons were deployed to the Gulf with a dedicated mission of clearing mines. This example is from HM-15 and is normally based at NAS Norfolk, VA. During Desert Shield/ Desert Storm, both squadrons flew from seaborne platforms and from Dhahran. (DOD)

Heavily committed to combat logistics, C-2A Greyhounds from VRC-30, 40 and 50, flew high priority cargo and personnel directly to the carriers. (Author)

In addition to the C-2A Greyhound, the US-3A, Viking also flew directly aboard the carriers. This Viking from VRC-50 is hauling cargo internally and externally in a huge underwing pod. (Rick Morgan)

An SH-3G, of HC-1, rests on the helicopter pad of the amphibious command ship USS Blue Ridge (LCC-19). This particular Sea King has been assigned to Vice Adm. Stanley R. Arthur, commander, Seventh Fleet. (Ensign Jeff Hilton USN)

The Kaman SH-3F Sea Sprite operated from a number of Frigates and Destroyers in the Persian Gulf and Red Sea. The type provided a limited attack capability as well as performing SAR and logistical duties. This example was assigned to HSL-34 and is lifting off from the flight deck of the USS Ticonderoga (CG-47). (PH2 Mark Kettenhoffen)

While operating primarily from Europe, the less heralded C-9B Skytrain II, moved high priority cargo and personnel to and from the theatre. (Marc Brouyere)

The EA-3B or "Whale" as it is affectionately known, was on station prior to the first strikes into Iraq. It provided invaluable information concerning the state of Iraqi air defenses and targeted SAM sites for USAF and USN HARM equipped aircraft. Of interest is the electronics "canoe" on the centerline of this EA-3B. This canoe housed a variety of antenna and ECM systems. (Cdr, Rick Burgess)

Fleet Air Reconnaissance Squadron Two, (VQ-2), deployed the last operational EA-3B Skywarriors to the Gulf region in November, 1990. Based at Jeddah, Saudi Arabia, they flew daily reconnaissance sorties monitoring the Iraq-Saudi border. During the air campaign the Skywarrior provided vital pre and post strike reconnaissance. (Cdr. Rick Burgess USN)

Following the invasion of Kuwait, the first combat capable US aircraft to arrive in the Gulf region were P-3C Orions of USN Patrol Squadron One, VP-1. These Orions deployed from Diego Garcia to Al Misirah Island, 11 miles off the coast of Oman. Within 48 hours of the invasion they were flying surveillance missions over the Gulf region. (Author)

In addition to the P-3C, other even lesser known Orions played a key role in the triumph of Desert Storm. The EP-3E, Aries II, Orion was based at Bahrain and Al Masirah. Two operational EP-3E squadrons, VQ-1 and 2 provided around-the-clock surveillance for carrier and land based strikes. These two squadrons were bolstered by other "uniquely" configured Orions from VPU-1 and 2. (PH3 Franklin P. Call USN)

The least reported upon aspect of the air campaign concerns the contributions made by the more than ten P-3 Squadrons which deployed aircraft and crews in support of Desert Shield/Desert Storm. Within hours of the start of Desert Storm, a P-3C, of VP-19, equipped with an over-the-horizon targeting system known as "Outlaw Hunter", formed a "lethal partnership" with F/A-18s and A-6s. The state-of-the-art systems in this prototype Orion yielded high quality targeting data which was passed along to strike aircraft. Orions teamed up with attack aircraft to sink or disable 53 of the 105 Iraqi ships destroyed during the war. (Ken Schmidt via David Reade)

Mission markings in the form of three Iraqi ships, applied to the nose gear door of P-3C, 159507. The markings attest to the Orions new ASUW (Antisurface Warfare) mission. (Ken Schmidt via David Reade)

UNITED STATES MARINE CORPS

The ground work for what would become the largest deployment of USMC aircraft ever attempted in a contingency operation was laid during the first week of August, 1990. Marine Air Group (MAG) 70, a quick reaction unit, was activated at MCAS El Toro as the advance force for 7th Marine Expeditionary Brigade, 1st Marine Expeditionary Force. On 12 August 1990, it deployed to Sheikh Isa, Bahrain. Upon arrival, MAG-70 rapidly became combat ready flying combat air patrols and training sorties to familiarize pilots with the terrain. By early September, its mission was accomplished and MAG-70 stood-down, being replaced by MAG-11 and Marine Air Wing (MAW)-3. A steady flow of Marine F/A-18 Hornets and A-6E Intruders continued to arrive through December 1990. In addition, the wing was further supplemented by four squadrons of KC-130 Hercules tankers and a squadron of electronic warfare EA-6B Prowlers. By the eve of the air campaign, MAG-11 had become the largest fighter and attack group in the Marine Corps.

In addition to the aircraft assigned to MAG-11, other USMC fixed-wing aircraft arrived in the Gulf region. These consisted of five AV-8B Harrier II squadrons supported by two squadrons of OV-10A/D Broncos. Designated MAG-13, this group was primarily shore based at Jubail Naval Base, one hundred miles from the Kuwait border. One additional squadron of Harriers, from VMA-331, deployed aboard the USS Nassau (LHA-4) as part of the 4th Marine Expeditionary Brigade and MAG-40. The remainder of USMC air groups, MAG-16, 26 and 50, consisted of rotary wing types such as the AH-1J/W, UH-1N, CH-46E, CH-53A/D/E and the RH-53D. The latter type was operated by Marine Unit HMH-772. CH-46's and CH-53's transported troops and equipment while the AH-1's and UH-1's acted in concert to provide close air support.

The air campaign began for the Marine Air Wings at 0440 hours 17 January 1991, when Marine A-6E Intruders, and F/A-18 Hornets, supported by KC-130 Hercules and EA-6B Prowlers, attacked Iraqi airfields and command and control centers. Harrier squadrons meanwhile, went about the task of preparing the battlefield for the ground offensive to follow. The USMC flew 17,770 combat sorties and delivered 20 million pounds of ordnance. Of this total, nearly 6,000 sorties were flown by USMC rotary wing aircraft.

MAG-11, the largest such unit assembled in Southwest Asia, was based at Shiekh Isa, Bahrain. This powerful Air Group was structured around the F/A-18 Hornet and the A-6E Intruder. (DOD)

A-6E, of VMA(AW)-224 following its return to MCAS Cherry Point NC. (Author)

The EA-6B Prowler is easily differentiated from the A-6E Intruder by its fin-tip pod, which houses a variety of antenna. The Prowler carries a crew of four, one pilot and three Electronic Countermeasures Officers (ECMO's). (Author)

Left: Bomb symbols on this A-6E of VMA(AW)-533 indicate it flew 51 combat missions. The turret below the nose houses the TRAM, or Target Recognition Attack Multi-sensor. USMC Intruders flew the majority of their missions at night utilizing TRAM generated images to identify targets. (Author)

A sample of mission markings typical of Intruders assigned to VMA(AW)-224. (Author)

During Desert Storm, USN and Marine EA-6Bs controlled the electronic battlefield. Unlike Navy Prowlers, the Marines Prowlers did not launch HARMs. This task was carried out by Marine Hornets and Intruders. This accounts for the absence of HARM silhouettes and the presence of lightening bolts on the nose of this VMAQ-2 Prowler. (Michael P. Kopack Sr.)

Right and below: Marine Fighter and Attack Squadron 232, the "Red Devil" squadron, traces its history to September, 1925. The Red Devil applied to this Hornet of VMFA-232, represented the most color viewed by this author on any Marine aircraft returning from the Gulf. (Author)

The Hornet element of MAG-11, deployed from MCAS Beaufort, SC, MCAS El Toro CA, and MCAS Kaneohe Bay, HI. A pair of VMFA-235 Hornets depart from MCAS Yuma on a training mission shortly after the war. (Author)

F/A-18 Hornet of MAG-11 "flys-the-basket" while refueling from a KC-135. This Hornet is carrying two AGM-88 HARMs used to suppress Iraqi air defenses. It also carried two wingtip mounted AIM-9 Sidewinders for self defense. (DOD)

VMFA-232 and 235 pilots go through final preflight checks prior to departing MCAS Beaufort on the next leg of an 11,000 mile flight to MCAS Kaneohe Bay Hawaii. (Author)

A Purple Heart commendation has been applied to this VMFA-451 Hornet. The ribbon is for the aircraft, not its pilot. This F/A-18A, 163141, survived a surface to air missile strike which impacted at its Sparrow missile station. (Author)

Two Hornet squadrons, VMFA-333 and 451, deployed from MCAS Beaufort to Sheikh Isa, "Shakie's Pizzia", Bahrain. VMFA-333, the "Shamrocks" was disestablished early in 1992. (Author)

Right and below: The first Marine squadron to reequip with the F/A-18 Hornet was VMFA-314. The unit was ordered to the Gulf from its base at MCAS El Toro, CA, during Desert Shield. Mission markings applied to this Hornet indicate it flew combat missions against tanks, APC's, mobile SAM launchers, artillery and a ship. (Author)

Another El Toro Hornet Squadron, the "Green Knights" of VMFA-121, was the first Marine unit to receive the F/A-18D. During the air campaign, the unit was tasked with the FASTFAC or Forward Air Control mission. This required the two man crews to locate and mark targets utilizing white phosphorous or 2.75 in rockets. (Author)

The 'Lancers' of VMFA-212 are one of three Hornet squadrons which deployed to the Gulf from MCAS Kaneohe Bay, HI. (Author)

To provide aerial refueling, the Marines dispatched all four of their KC-130 squadrons to Bahrain, basing the Hercules tankers at Jubail and Sheikh ISA. A KC-130F from VMGR-352 is shown. (Author)

Lifting off on another refueling mission is a KC-130T, of Marine Corps reserve squadron VMGR-452. (Author)

The CITY OF YUMA, a UC-12B, Huron, from MCAS Yuma, was utilized along with other examples of the type to provide intra-theatre transportation during Desert Shield/Desert Storm. (Author)

This Iraqi Bell 214SP helicopter was captured by the 1st Marine Division at Kuwait Intl. Airport, 27 February 1991. It was transported to MCAS El Toro and is currently displayed as part of that base's impressive air museum. (Author)

As was the norm among returning Harrier squadrons, VMA-231 did not carry an abundance of special markings. In fact, this squadron returned with the greatest amount of mission markings compared to other Harrier units. "Venom" was the VMA-231, commander's aircraft. (Author)

Capt. Rich 'Hiney' Linnekin poses with his Harrier. He deployed to the Gulf region from Iwakuni, Japan, which had to be one of the longest deployments of the war. (Author)

"Free Kuwait" is written in Arabic on the side of this AV-8B of VMA-231. USMC Harriers played a significant role in doing just that by delivering 5.9 million pounds of ordnance during the Gulf war. Mission markings on this aircraft indicate it contributed 70 combat missions to the war effort. (Author)

MCAS Cherry Point Harriers returned with a variety of different paint schemes. These were often the result of paints mixed in 55 gallon drums. No two Harriers were painted exactly alike. (Author)

AV-8B of VMFA-231, taxis out with a light load of six MK-82, 500lb, general purpose bombs. MAG-13 Harriers operated out of King Abdul Aziz Naval Base and from Forward Operating Locations such as Tanajob. (Author)

No two Harriers of VMA-542 appeared to be painted or marked the same. This example is the squadron commanders aircraft and is overall gray with the name "Babieca" on its side. (Author)

This VMA-542 attrition replacement was drawn from VMAT-203, the Harrier training squadron based at MCAS Cherry Point. This AV-8B carries the dual markings for both VMA-542 and VMAT-203. (Author)

AV-8B of VMA-542, displaying yet another Gulf paint scheme variation. This scheme is currently being phased out in favor of a two tone gray scheme. (Author)

AV-8B Harrier IIs of VMA-542 deployed to the Gulf region via a trans-Atlantic flight supported by USAF tankers. An AV-8B, with refueling probe extended approaches a tanker over the Atlantic. (DOD)

VMA-311, from MCAS Yuma AZ, was one of four Harrier squadrons based at King Abdul Aziz Naval Base. A total of four Harriers were downed by enemy action, the majority by heat seeking missiles. Tactics employed by Harrier squadrons required they come within range of shoulder fired SAMs and anti-aircraft fire. (Author)

The OV-10 Bronco was developed during the Vietnam war as a counterinsurgency aircraft. Two Marine squadrons, VMO-1 and 2, equipped with the OV-10A and the improved version the OV-10D, deployed to the Gulf aboard USN carriers and were flown off when they entered the Gulf region. Although the type possessed a high degree of maneuverability, its use was limited in the high threat environment of the KTO. Both USMC Bronco units have since been deactivated. (MAP)

In an attempt to lessen its vulnerability to ground fire, several Broncos, such as this OV-10A of VMO-2, were repainted in a two-tone desert scheme. Both Bronco losses in Desert Storm were OV-10A's. The first, 155435, assigned to VMO-2 was brought down on 18 January 1991. The second, 155424, assigned to VMO-1 was downed by a shoulder-fired SAM on 25 February 1991. (Robert L. Lawson)

Unmanned Aerial Vehicles, or UAVs, played a key role in the Gulf war. They were used extensively in exposing Iraqi air defenses, spotting troop concentrations and mapping routes through Iraqi ground defenses. This Pioneer UAV represents one of the earlier models deployed to the Gulf. (DOD)

Hellfire equipped "Whiskey" Cobra gunships, similar to this AH-1W, were used to good effect in breaking the back of the surprise Iraqi thrust into Khafji. (DOD)

AH-1 Cobra Gunships teamed with UH-1N Hueys to make the difference on more than one occasion, ensuring success for the Marine advance on Kuwait City. (DOD)

The charred remains of British Airways 747, G-AWND. Next to it lay the remains of a Kuwait Air Force C-9. Both were destroyed during Coalition air strikes on the Kuwait International Airport while it was in Iraqi hands. (DOD)

This AH-1W, or "Whiskey Cobra" in Marine parlance, carries six APC kill markings just aft of the gunner's cockpit. This example served with HMLA-369, MAG-16 during the Gulf war. (Author)

Right and below: Sea Knights similar to these CH-46Es of HMM-161, were shore based at Abdul Aziz Naval Base, Saudi Arabia. This USMC workhorse was used extensively to move troops and equipment to the front. Of interest are the paint scheme variations on these two Sea Knights. (MAP)

A CH-46E of HMM-165, lands aboard the USS Missouri in the Persian Gulf. Two Marine Sea Knights were destroyed during the war under non-combat circumstances. (DOD)

Though officially named the Iroquois, this UH-1N and others like it are fondly referred to as 'Hueys.' This example is armed with rockets. The type was quite effective in providing close air support alongside Cobra gunships. (MAP)

At least four different paint schemes were worn by CH-53D/Es of MAG-16. Besides hauling troops, the Sea Stallion airlifted respectable loads of cargo to the front. (MAP)

Three CH-53Ds of HMH-463 cross the desert at low level while on a Desert Shield training mission. Of interest is the unit code "YH", applied to the fuselage. It is normally carried on the tail assembly. Note the contrast between the paint schemes. (USMC)

CH-53E, Super Stallion of Marine Heavy Helicopter Squadron 464 (HMH-464), warms up on the flight deck of the amphibious transport USS Raleigh (LPD-1). The paint scheme was later altered with an additional shade of gray to cover the dark green. (Capt. Rick Mullen)

Left and two below: MAG-26 Cobras, Sea Knights and Super Stallions, were instrumental in capturing the Kuwait International Airport. Pictured here from top to bottom, AH-1J, HMA-775; CH-46E, HMM-266; and CH-53E, HMH-464. (MAP)

The USN transferred its last RH-53D to the Marines on 10 April 1990. Prior to Marine service, the type flew with HM-14 as a mine countermeasure aircraft. During Desert Storm, RH-53Ds served with HMH-772, a Marine Reserve unit. The type is most famous for the April 1980 hostage rescue attempt in Iran. The RH-53Ds aerial refueling capability greatly enhanced its value during the Gulf war. (Keith Snyder)

Close up of markings on RH-53D, 158689, of HMH-772. (Keith Snyder)

The standard Marine Land Camouflage of blue gray, field green and black proved to be inappropriate for warfare in the desert. Vic Duniec, a CH-46 Sea Knight pilot assigned to HMM-261, proposed a new scheme consisting of blue gray over light compass grey. The scheme was based upon the USN and Marines "counter-shaded" camouflage used on fixed-wing aircraft. This CH-46E, of HMM-774 was photographed after the war at NAS Norfolk still wearing this obviously effective scheme. Of interest is the applique armor near its engines. (Author)

Based aboard the USS Raleigh (LPD-1), this CH-46E of HMM-263 displays some unusual nose art. (DOD)

AV-8B of VMA-331, shortly after returning from the Gulf war. VMA-331 was the only fixed-wing squadron assigned to MAG-40. The squadron lost one Harrier, 162740, on 27 February 1991. (Kevin Foy)

"Whiskey Cobra" of HMLA-269 following its return from the Gulf. The AH-1W is equipped with an M-197 20mm cannon. It can also carry a variety of ordnance including TOW, Hellfire and Sidewinder missiles and an assortment of unguided rockets. (Author)

CH-46E of HMM-263 in a very war weary paint scheme. (Author)

On 25 February, 1991, elements of the 4th MEB, including this CH-46E of HMM-365, were highly successful in tying down several Iraqi divisions with an assault feint along the Kuwaiti Peninsula. (Barry Roop)

This ALQ-156, Infrared countermeasures jammer is one means of self-defense employed by Marine helicopters deployed to the Gulf. Helicopters also relied on chaff and flare dispensers to defeat SAMs. (Jeff Rankin-Lowe/ Sirius)

Significant numbers of the "Huey" still equip Marine attack squadrons such as HMLA-269. The UH-1N's utilized during Desert Storm were teamed with AH-J/W's to provide close air support for Marine ground forces. (Author)

CH-53E, KAMEL KRUZERS of HMH-461, aboard the USS Trenton. (CW4 John Lawson)

CH-53E, THE DIRTY DOZEN, of HMH-461, is seen here touching down aboard the USS Iwo Jima (LPH-2), during Desert Storm. Of interest is the other all green paint scheme. (CWO Ed Bailey)

SONIC YOUTH GOO, appeared on the side of an unidentified CH-53E of HMH-461. (CW4 John Lawson)

"In the Mood", HMH-461, photographed aboard the USS Iwo Jima, (LPH-2). (CW4 John Lawson)

Comic strip characters "Calvin and Hobbes" go to war with HMH-461 aboard a CH-53E. Of interest is the gray paint which appears to have been applied by brush or roller. Many Marine helicopters were hastily painted prior to or just after reaching the Gulf region. (CW4 John Lawson)

Once the ground war commenced, Marine Super Stallions were used quite extensively hauling troops, cargo and even fuel to Forward Operating Locations (FOLs). (CWO2 Ed Bailey, USNR)

Thirty examples of the twin "Huey" UH-1N were deployed to the Gulf region during the war. This example is from HMLA-169 and was deployed aboard ship in the Persian Gulf throughout much of the war. (Author)

AH-1W, positioned aboard ship somewhere in the Persian Gulf. (MAP)

During the Gulf war, HU-25B Falcon jets from Cape Cod, utilized Aireye side-looking airborne radar in addition to its infrared sensors to plot the course of a massive oil spill unleashed by Iraqi forces occupying Kuwait. (USCG)

U.S. Army

Private James Carlson, 82nd Airborne Division, performs maintenance on the rotar of an OH-58 Kiowa. The OH-58 was used extensively during the Gulf War working as scouts and Forward air controllers for Army Apaches and USMC AH-1W Cobras. (MSgt. Bill Thompson)

UH-60A Black Hawks of the 82nd Airborne Division airlift M-102, 105mm Howitzers. (Brian Cumper)

The CH-47 Chinook is the Army's heavy lift helicopter, and was employed during the Gulf War in moving troops and heavy equipment. The type was utilized by the 101st Airborne Division to spearhead its ground offensive. (Keith Snyder)

UH-60A, L and V Black Hawks were seldom called upon for medevac duties due to the low casualty rates. The type nevertheless was responsible for saving many lives. (Robert F. Dorr)

A fleet of UH-60A Black hawks similar to this example were used to fly three Air Assault Infantry Brigades into the Nasiriyah area of Iraq prior to the start of the ground war. (DOD)

Introduced to combat nearly thirty years ago during the Vietnam conflict, the UH-1 'Huey', saw widespread service during Desert Shield and Desert Storm. This example from the Texas National Guard was painted in a Desert camouflage scheme by British troops in exchange for a couple hundred pounds of bacon. (Peter Wilson)

This AH-1F Cobra gunship was one of twenty-one deployed to the Gulf region by the 101st Airborne Division. Of interest is the name 'Sand Shark' painted near the engine access panels. (MAP)

The opening shots of the air war were fired by AH-64A Apache helicopters similar to this example. Armed with AGM-114 Hellfire missiles and 30mm chain gun, Apaches destroyed two Iraqi early warning sites on the morning of 17 January 1991. (DOD)

This RC-12D, of the 1st Military Intelligence Battalion, is normally based at Wiesbaden, Germany. During the Gulf War, the 1st MIB provided crucial reconnaissance and intelligence information to ground troops, particularly during the 100 hour ground war. (Scott Van Aken)

This RU-21H, 'Guard Rail' version of the Beech King Air was assigned to the 224th MIB during the Gulf War. The type was used extensively in gathering intelligence and in performing reconnaissance on the tactical level. (Peter Wilson)

C-23B, 88-1866, BART-66, was assigned to the Alabama National Guard. This unit was the only one of its type to deploy the C-23B, or Sherpa, from the continental United States. Of interest are the chaff and flare dispensers which were added to the vertical stabilizers prior to deployment. (Joe Zerbe)

Right and below: A total of forty-two Mohawks were deployed in support of Desert Shield/Desert Storm. The majority were based at Riyad, Saudi Arabia. The type was used extensively, flying around-the-clock SIGINT and ELINT missions. Mohawks were also successful in hunting and locating SCUDS and Battle Damage Assessment. This example was assigned to the 2nd Military Intelligence Battalion which has since been disbanded. Of interest are the mission markings in the form of camels applied to the nose gear door. (Alfredo Maglione via JEM Slides)

A number of Army C-12/Ds were utilized during the Gulf War to transport Army officials through the theatre. (Scott Van Aken)

Better known to the public as J-STARS, the E-8, Joint Surveillance/Target Attack Radar System is a highly modified Boeing 707-300. The E-8 is equipped with a Multi-Mode Pulse Doppler Radar which can produce photographic-like images of fixed targets. The J-STARS Synthetic Aperture Radar can pinpoint moving targets. During Desert Storm, two E-8s were utilized and flew forty-nine combat missions, each averaging 10.5 hours in duration. (Randy Jolly)

OPERATION GRANBY – RAF

Following the Iraqi invasion of Kuwait, the Royal Air Force immediately began to plan for the eventual deployment of forces to Southwest Asia. On 11 August 1990, Tornado F.3 interceptors began to arrive in Saudi Arabia from RAF Akrotiri, Cyprus. Their arrival commenced Britain's largest military operation since World War II. This initial deployment was followed by Jaguars and Nimrod maritime patrol aircraft. On 29 August 1990, the ground attack variant of the Tornado, the GR.1, began to arrive in the Gulf region. Detachments of GR.1's were soon established at Muharraq Bahrain, in addition to Tabuk and Dhahran in Saudi Arabia. Three versions of RAF tankers, the Victor K.2, VC-10 K.2/3 and the TriStar K.1, supported the movement of aircraft, troops and equipment to the Gulf. Intra-theatre transportation was carried out by RAF C-130 Hercules. A detachment of two Royal New Zealand C-130H's from 40 squadron shuttled between the UK and the Gulf in support of RAF operations.

A substantial fleet of helicopters was also dispatched to the Gulf in support of the two armored brigades which consisted of 30,000 men. The Royal Navy, RAF and Army Air Corps contributed Lynx, Sea King, Puma Gazelle and Chinook helicopters.

During the early morning hours of 17 January 1991, Tornado GR.1's, flying low and utilizing the JP223 Runway Denial Weapon, spearheaded attacks against Iraqi airfields. During the first week of the air campaign, five Tornado GR.1's were lost to enemy action, attesting to the risks involved in this type of mission. Meanwhile, RAF Jaguars went about the task of Battlefield Air Interdiction in southern Kuwait. With the commencement of the ground war, emphasis was switched to Republican Guard positions in northern Kuwait. Jaguars, or 'Desert Cats' as they became known, delivered 1,000-lb. bombs, cluster bombs and rockets. No precision guided ordnance was delivered by RAF Jaguars. The introduction of the Buccaneer S.2B coincided with the achievement of air supremacy over Iraq. Utilizing the AVQ-23E Pave Spike pod, Buccaneers illuminated targets for LGB carrying Tornados. Late in the air campaign, Buccaneers delivered 1,000-lb. Paveway II LGBs, primarily against bridges and airfields.

In the Persian Gulf, RN Lynx helicopters armed with Sea Skua anti-ship missiles played a significant role in the destruction of the Iraqi Navy, claiming 15 ships sunk. This figure included five TNC-45-class attack craft capable of launching Exocet anti-ship missiles. RN Sea Kings, deployed to the Gulf aboard the casualty-clearing ship, RFA Argus. These were intended for medical evacuation, but instead were camouflaged desert pink and accompanied troops near the front lines. These Sea Kings were joined by RAF Pumas and took part in moving men and material during the ground war. Meanwhile, Chinook HC.1's were committed to logistical duties and towards the end of the conflict, moving POWs. Rotary wing attack was carried out by British Army Gazelles which served as scouts for TOW-equipped Lynx helicopters. The pair formed a lethal partnership responsible for the destruction of a number of Iraqi armored vehicles.

Two Tornado GR.1's participate in low level training prior to Operation Desert Storm. The Tornado in the foreground is from 20 squadron and his wingman is from 15 squadron. (Flt. Lt. Stuart Osbourne RAF)

A Tornado GR.1, from 15 squadron taxis in following a sortie. All RAF ground attack variants of the Tornado were camouflaged in a desert paint scheme. In addition, the majority of these returned from the Gulf with impressive nose art and mission markings. Of interest is the SkyShadow ECM pod mounted on the outboard wing station. (MAP)

Below: SNOOPY AIRWAYS appeared on the right side of several Muhurraq based Tornados. This example, ZA491/N, from 20 squadron carried NIKKI and impressive mission markings on its left side. (Robbie Shaw)

Above left: MISS BEHAVIN, adorned 17 squadron Tornado, ZA374/CN. Early in the war, this Tornado appeared briefly with a CNN tail code. The Palm Tree mission markings indicate missions flown from Dhahran. (Robbie Shaw)

Above: American cartoon character "Garfield" flew with 15 squadron aboard Tornado GR.1, ZA463/Q. (John Grech)

Left: An impressive combination of mission markings, nose art and sharks-mouth appeared on 16 squadron Tornado GR.1 ZA465/FK. (John Grech)

CHECK SIX, Tornado GR.1 ZD719/AD, of 9 squadron. Of interest are the external fuel tanks common to the F.3 version of the Tornado. (Bob Archer)

AWESOME ANNIE, . . . ah . . . clutches a bomb on Tornado GR.1 ZD809/BA. In addition to this 14 squadron Tornado, many others carried the legend "Hello Kuwait G'bye Iraq."

ANNA LOUISE. Tornado GR.1 ZD715/AL, of 9 squadron.

GULF KILLER, Tornado GR.1 ZA452/GK of 20 squadron prominently displayed are ten smart bomb silhouettes indicating it may have been teamed with a Pave Spike equipped Buccaneer. (Andy Thomson)

A total of six dedicated reconnaissance Tornados were deployed to the Gulf. The reconnaissance version has been modified with an Infra-red Linescan System, Side Looking Airborne Radar and video recorders. This particular Tornado flew 18 recce missions during the war. (via Sergio Bottaro)

MIG EATER, Tornado GR.1 ZA447/EA from 15 squadron. The MiG kill marking denotes a MiG-29 Fulcrum destroyed as it was on final approach to an airfield under attack by Tornados. Early reports indicate that this Tornado emptied its JP223 Runway Denial Weapon as it flew over the landing Fulcrum. (Bob Archer)

ANOLA KAY, Tornado GR.1 ZD748/AK from 9 squadron. This example was one of a handful of RAF Tornados equipped to launch the ALARM Anti-Radar Missile. Of interest are the ALARM silhouettes painted under the windscreen. (Robbie Shaw)

The F.3 is the dedicated interceptor version of the Tornado. It is easily distinguished from the GR.1 by its elongated nose which houses the AI-24 Foxhunter radar. Number 29 squadron, which traces its history to World War I, was deployed to Dhahran Saudi Arabia along with 43 squadron. Of interest are the 495 gallon fuel tanks referred to as "Hindenbergers." (Author)

ARMOURED CHARMER, Tornado GR.1, ZD739/AC, from 9 squadron, was one of five TIALD equipped Tornados deployed to the Gulf. TIALD, or Thermal Imaging And Laser Designation, made its debute during Desert Storm. A number of the 350 hardened shelters destroyed during the war were destroyed by TIALD equipped Tornados. (Robbie Shaw)

Jaguars were the first RAF combat aircraft deployed to the Gulf. This example is from 41 squadron, which was taking part in the Reconnaissance Air Meet at Bergstrom AFB., Texas, when the order to deploy was issued.

Deployed to Muharraq, Bahrain in October 1990, RAF Jaguars such as this war weary example, flew 618 combat sorties during Desert Storm. Of interest is the placement of the Sidewinder launch rail, above the wing. (Robbie Shaw)

Several Jaguars wore nose art from a popular British adult comic book, "VIZ." Characters carried on RAF Jaguars included: JOHNNY FARTPANTS, on XX725; BUSTER GONAD . . ., XZ118; and FAT SLAGS, XX962. (XX725 and XX962, Bob Archer) (XZ118, Robbie Shaw)

KATRINA JANE, Jaguar GR.1A, XZ119/Z, is a perfect example of RAF Gulf war nose art and mission markings. (Bob Archer)

A caricature of Squadron Leader Bagshaw in a pink Spitfire adorned the side of Jaguar GR.1A XX733/R. (Robbie Shaw)

The name of a popular British periodical, "The Guardian Reader" was applied to Jaguar GR.1A XZ375/S. (Robbie Shaw)

MARY ROSE, Jaguar GR.1A, XZ356/N. Of interest are the mission markings which consist of bombs, cameras and rockets. (Andy Thomson)

The name Debbie originally appeared on this Jaguar, XZ367/P. Subsequently, the name was replaced with a simple white rose. (Andy Thomson)

SADMAN gets a well deserved British boot on Jaguar GR.1A, XZ364/Q.

Buccaneer S.2B, XV863/S, SEA WITCH, is representative of the outstanding artwork of Cpl. Kenny Letham, a member of 208 squadron. (Robbie Shaw)

DIPLOMATIC SERVICE, adorning Jaguar GR.1A, XZ358/W, represents the state of undress displayed by the majority of RAF nose art viewed on RAF fighter aircraft returning from the Gulf war. (John Grech)

Buccaneer S.2B's arrived at Muharraq Bahrain on 26 January 1991. The type was used to illuminate targets utilizing the AN/AVQ-23E Pave Spike Pod. (Bob Archer)

THE FLYING MERMAID adorned Buccaneer S.2B, XX901/N. Mission markings consist of 'smart bombs' and an Iraqi AN-12 destroyed on the ground during the final day of the conflict. (Robbie Shaw)

DIRTY HARRIET, Buccaneer S.2B, XV332, was prepared for Gulf war service complete with desert pink paint and nose art. The conflict concluded before this particular Buccaneer could be deployed. (Andy Thomson)

The Buccaneer crews and support personnel were often referred to as the "Desert Pirates" or as "Sky Pirates." The "Jolly-Roger" flag was prominently displayed on the left side of all Buccaneers deployed to the Gulf. (John Grech)

One of the most provocative forms of nose art appeared on HELLO SAILOR, Buccaneer, S.2B, XX885/L. The name "Famous Grouse" is a brand of Scottish whiskey. (Bob Archer)

MISS JOLLY ROGER, Buccaneer, S.2B, XW533/A, is a far cry from the nose art appearing on U.S. aircraft. Some examples of Buccaneer nose art survived for some time after the war. (Robbie Shaw)

Another Gulf war veteran scheduled for retirement was the Victor K.2. Eight Victors from 55 Squadron deployed to the Gulf and operated primarily from Muharraq Bahrain. The type was tasked with refueling RAF and other Coalition fighter aircraft. (Bob Archer)

Victor K.2, XH671, was originally titled SLINKY SUE; this was later changed to SWEET SUE. (Robbie Shaw)

Typical mission markings carried by Victor K.2s were rows of gas pumps. (Bob Archer)

Six of the eight Victor K.2's deployed to the Gulf returned with nose art. LUCKY LOU, on XM717, is a typical example of the outstanding artwork displayed by Victors. (Andy Thomson)

Victor K.2, XM672, MAID MARIAN. (Robbie Shaw)

Victor K.2, XL231, LUSTY LINDY. (Robbie Shaw)

Victor K.2, XM715, TEASIN TINA. (MAP)

Victor K.2, XL164, SAUCY SAL. (Robbie Shaw)

Mission markings in the form of Tornado silhouettes and the inscription "The Empire Strikes Back", adorn the side of a 101 squadron VC-10 K.3. (Robbie Shaw)

A VC-10 K.3, tanker of 101 squadron refuels a brace of Tornado F.3 interceptors. Nine VC-10s were divided between Seeb Oman, Muharraq Bahrain and Riyadh Saudi Arabia. The VC-10 K.2/3 flew in support of RAF strike missions.

The majority of TriStar K.1's of 216 squadron operated from RAF Brize Norton during Desert Shield/Desert Storm. However, two were painted in desert pink and flew refueling missions from Muharraq Bahrain. Due to their portly appearance and pink scheme, these two TriStars were dubbed the "Pink Pigs." (Robbie Shaw)

RAF Hercules were heavily committed to transporting troops and equipment throughout the Gulf Theatre of Operations. The type holds the distinction of being the first coalition fixed wing aircraft to land at Kuwait City Airport following its recapture. (Robbie Shaw)

RAF Hercules were supplemented by a pair of Royal New Zealand C-130H's of 40 squadron. The type flew shuttle missions between the UK and Gulf region. (R.A. London)

Nimrod MR.2P's were committed to search and rescue and maritime patrol missions. The latter role was in support of the UN backed naval blockade of Iraq. (Robbie Shaw)

The Special Operations R.1P Nimrods of 51 squadron are rarely photographed. This example, cruising above the British countryside, saw extensive service in the Gulf providing "special services." (Robbie Shaw)

Number 32 squadron dispatched a handful of BAe 125's to the Gulf region to serve as VIP transports. (Robbie Shaw)

A Puma HC.1 similar to this example from 33 squadron, RAF, was the first aircraft to land in Kuwait City following its liberation. (Robbie Shaw)

A Chinook HC.1 of 7 squadron displays white Coalition recognition markings. The inverted chevron (actually an Arabic 8), was carried by all Coalition vehicles associated with the ground war. (Robbie Shaw)

A few Chinooks, such as this HC.1 of 7 squadron, were used in nocturnal operations requiring their desert schemes be toned down with liberal amounts of dark paint. (Andy Thomson)

Westland Sea King HC.4 of 846 Naval Air Sqaudron. The type was utilized primarily as a troop carrier and medevac helicopter during the ground war. (Frank McMeiken via Sergio Bottaro)

In order to afford some protection from the fine sand of the Gulf region, Royal Navy Sea Kings, such as this example from 848 squadron were fitted with engine inlet filters. During the ground war, 848 squadron Sea Kings, supported the 1st British Armored Division and moved more than 50 miles into Iraq with the division. (MAP)

The Royal Navy Lynx HAS.3 was the first helicopter to become directly involved in action in the Gulf. The type was tasked with enforcing the UN naval blockade against Iraq and escorted a number of boarding parties prior to the commencement of the shooting war. Once Desert Storm began, Lynx HAS.3's worked closely with USN attack aircraft, utilizing its Sea Spray radar for over-the-horizon targeting of Iraqi ships. (Frank McMeiken via Sergio Bottaro)

British Army Air Corps Lynx AH.7 helicopters, armed with TOW anti-tank missiles were utilized at night via the use of night-vision goggles and infra-red sighting system. Teamed with Gazelle helicopters, the trio proved quite successful in destroying Iraqi armor. (Robbie Shaw)

The Army Air Corp Gazelles were used primarily as scouts for TOW equipped Lynx helicopters. (Robbie Shaw)

OPERATION FRICTION

The Canadian Armed Forces effort to support Desert Shield/Desert Storm began with the deployment of six highly modified CH-124A Sea King helicopters. These Sea Kings were embarked aboard ships of Canadian Task Group 302.3, which departed from Halifax, Nova Scotia on 24 August 1990. By 1 October, the first CAF Sea King patrols were being flown in the Gulf region. Shortly thereafter they commenced escorting boarding parties in support of the UN embargo against Iraq.

The nucleus of the Canadian contribution consisted of CF-188A Hornets which began arriving in the Gulf region on 7 October 1990. These Hornets were flying CAP sorties within two days from Doha AB., Qatar. The CAF detachment shared these facilities with Qatari Air Force Mirage F.1s, USAF F-16C Falcons from the 401st TFW and French Air Force Mirage F.1s. This initial deployment of CF-188A's consisted of 409 squadron from CFB Baden-Soellingen, Germany. In mid-December 409 squadron was replaced by aircraft and personnel drawn from 416 and 439 squadron. Additional Hornets drawn from 441 squadron brought the total number to twenty-four. This figure was later increased to twenty-six. Personnel were employed from 409, 410, 421 and 441 squadrons in addition to those of 416 and 439 squadron. Aerial refueling was provided by a single CC-137 of 437 squadron.

Primarily tasked with performing Combat Air Patrol in the Central Gulf, the mission of the CAF Hornets was later expanded to include sweep and escort duties. During the later stages of the air campaign, prior to the ground war, CAF Hornets were authorized to conduct missions against ground targets including Republican Guard positions and later the escape route used by the retreating Iraqi Army.

The snowy landscape indicates this CF-188A was not photographed in the Gulf. Instead, it was photographed at the London Ontario Int. Apt., shortly after the conclusion of Operation Desert Storm. This particular Hornet, 188741, along with 188798, attacked an Iraqi TNC-45 patrol boat. After strafing the craft several times, one CF-188A launched an AIM-7M Sparrow which impacted 50 feet from the boat. This TNC-45 was later finished off by USN Intruders. Both participating CF-188A's received ship kill markings for the role they played in the attack and the crafts subsequent destruction. (Mike Reyno)

Taxying out for a CAP mission, this CF-188A is armed with the standard CAP load of four AIM-7 Sparrows and four AIM-9 Sidewinders. CAF Hornets were initially tasked with protecting coalition warships from attack by Exocet carrying Iraqi fighters. (Michael P. Kopack Jr.)

During the first two weeks of the air campaign, the single CAF, CC-137 tanker deployed to the Gulf region, transferred over two million pounds of fuel. The type not only refueled CAF Hornets, but also attended to the needs of USMC and USN fighters as well. On the second day of the war a pair of F-14 Tomcats, dangerously low on fuel, were saved by the 437 Squadron CC-137, CAF. (Mike Reyno)

Two CC-144 Challengers of 414 squadron deployed to Bahrain and were utilized for liaison and communications flights within the Gulf region. (Mike Reyno)

A CC-130E Hercules of the Canadian Armed Forces leaps into the air during a flight demonstration at the London Ontario International Air Show, 2 June 1991. CAF Hercules were very active during Desert Shield/ Desert Storm ferrying troops and material throughout the region. Following the war, CAF Hercules continued to fly supply missions in northern Iraq following the Kurdish uprising. (Author)

A smiling feline named LUCK LOUIE, appears on Sea King 12413 of CAF Helicopter Squadron HS-423. (Jeff Rankin-Lowe/Sirius)

This HS-423 Sea King, 12412, was named HORMUZ HUMPER. Of interest is the Operation Friction badge depicting a Sea King over the Persian Gulf and the inscription "KA-BLAM SADDAM" written below it. (Chris Aleong)

Canadian Armed Forces Sea Kings were highly modified prior to their deployment to the Gulf. Modifications included Flare and Chaff dispensers, radar warning receivers, Global Positioning receiver, additional armor, search radar and Forward Looking Infra-Red (FLIR). (Mike Reyno)

OPERATION DAGUET

On 15 September 1990, French President Francois Mitterrand dispatched fighters to Saudi Arabia. This deployment was the vanguard for a larger movement of French personnel and aircraft known as Operation Daguet. The first French fighter aircraft to arrive in the region consisted of 4 Mirage 2000C's of the 5th Escadre de Chasse and 4 Mirage F. CR's of the 33rd Escadre de Reconnaissance. These were supported by C-135FR tankers from the 93rd Escadre de Ravitaillement. All French fighter aircraft were based at AlAhsa which is situated east of Riyadh Saudi Arabia. The C-135FRs and other French transport aircraft established a base of operations at Riyadh. Within a week of its arrival this force was bolstered by additional Mirage 2000C's and F.1CR's. It was further strengthened in October with the arrival of Jaguars from 11th Escadre de Chasse, Puma SAR helicopters and an electronics surveillance C-160G Gabriel of 54 Escadron Electronique. By the eve of Desert Storm, the French Air Force had 51 aircraft in the Gulf region.

When the air campaign commenced, the French Air Force was tasked with providing the second wave of attack aircraft on the first night of the war. The lead elements of this second wave consisted of Jaguars attacking the Ahmed Al Jaber AB., at very low level. Four Jaguars from this force were subsequently damaged by Iraqi air defenses. Follow up missions were conducted at higher altitudes utilizing AS-30L laser guided missiles and BLG-66 sub-munitions. Throughout the conflict, French Jaguars attacked airfields, ammunition depots, naval bases and Republican Guard positions.

The Mirage 2000C interceptors of the 5th Escadre de Chasse flew CAP missions armed with Magic 520D and Magic 2 air-to-air missiles. Initially tasked to protect high value targets, these Mirages began to escort French Jaguars into Iraqi airspace during the second week of the war. Meanwhile, the French Mirage F.1CR, did not fly its first combat missions until 26 January, after the Coalition had achieved air supremacy. This was due to the fact that Iraq possessed Mirage F. 1EQ's which were nearly identical in appearance to the French F.1CR. The F.1CR's of the 33rd Escadre de Reconnaissance bombed Iraqi positions in Kuwait and Iraq and utilized their Raphael Side Looking Airborne Radar (SLAR) to gather reconnaissance and post strike imagery.

The deployment of French Air Force units to the Gulf and their subsequent use in combat required the establishment of an air bridge between France and the Gulf. This mission was accomplished by C-160 Transalls and a single C-130 Hercules. The deployment was further supplemented by Air France 747's. Aerial refueling for the deployment was carried out by five C-135FRs. During the air war, the French Air Force flew 1,387 combat missions without the loss of a single aircraft. The bulk of these missions were flown by the C-135FR's.

Mirage F.1CR's of the 33rd Escadre de Reconnaissance were some of the first French Air Force combat aircraft to arrive in the Gulf region.

Equipped with a Cyrano IV, MR Multi-Mode radar, the French Mirage F.1CR, was capable of flying in all types of weather. This example from 1/33 "Belfort" Escadron.

This Mirage F.1CR from 2/33 "Savoie" escadron, was not committed to combat operations until 26 January 1991. This was due to the similarity between it and Iraqi Mirage F.1EQ's.

Shortly after their arrival at Al Ahsa airport, Mirage 2000C's of the 5th Escadre de Chasse began flying CAP missions. Although a few Mirage 2000C's were repainted in a desert camouflage scheme, the majority retained their European schemes while deployed to the Gulf.

This Jaguar A from 1/11th "Roussillon" escadron in desert markings was photographed shortly after its return to France following Operation Desert Storm.

War weary example of a Jaguar A from 3/11 "Corse" escadron. The store is a Phimat decoy launcher. French Air Force Jaguars and pilots entered the Gulf war with combat experience gained in Africa during Operations Manta and Epervier where they conducted air strikes against Libyan backed rebels. (C. Boisselon via Sergio Bottaro)

Jaguar A from 4/11 "Jura" escadron. Mounted on the center-line is a Atlis Illuminator pod which was used in conjunction with AS-30L laser guided missiles. The 4th escadron of the 11th Escadre de Chasse was disbanded in July 1992.

Aerial refueling for French aircraft was provided by the C-135FR. The type very closely resembles the USAF KC-135R. The French Air Force utilizes the hose and drogue method of aerial refueling. (Charles T. Robbins)

Transalls such as this example from the 61st Escadre de Transport can haul 16 tons of freight. The pace of the French deployment was such that Air France 747's (capable of carrying a single load equivalent to that of ten Transalls) were pressed into service. (Authors Collection)

A pair of Puma SA-330 helicopters of the 1/67th "pyrennes" escadron deployed to Al Ahsa to conduct Search and Rescue operations. Late in the war, one of these French Pumas was successful in rescuing a USN pilot downed deep inside Kuwait.

OPERATION LOCUSTO

The Italian contribution to Desert Shield/Desert Storm consisted of twelve Tornados drawn from 6, 36 and 50 Stormo. These aircraft underwent modifications which included updated cooling systems, sand filters and a new desert pink paint scheme. The deployment was supported by a C-130 and G-222 transport. The entire Italian contingent was based at Abu Dhabi AB., Al Dhafra United Arab Emirates.

During the air campaign, Italian Tornados flew 226 sorties and delivered 565 1,000-lb general purpose bombs. The most notable mission was the first. On 18 January 1991, eight Italian Tornados launched for an attack on an Iraqi airfield. One withdrew due to a mechanical problem. Six of the remaining aircraft were unsuccessful in refueling from a USAF KC-135. The only Tornado which managed to refuel, pressed on with the attack. This lone Tornado, MM7074, of 50 Stormo, was subsequently shot down during the attack.

In addition to Tornados, the Italian Air Force dispatched a handful of RF/F-104G Starfighters from 3 Stormo. These were deployed to Turkey after that country requested military assistance from fellow NATO members in order to secure its border with Iraq.

Italian Tornados of 6 Stormo photographed shortly after it returned from the Gulf. The missile-like object on the outboard wing pylon is a BOZ-107 Counter Measures Dispenser pod.

Following an inauspicious debut to the air war, Italian Tornados were divided into four bombers and four aerial refuelers. This example carries a center-line 'buddy-store' refueling pod, an ECM pod and AIM-9 Sidewinder.

Italian Air Force RF/F-104G Starfighters from 28 Squadron, 3rd Wing were deployed to Turkey as part of the AMF or ACE Mobile Force. The Starfighter deployment was in response to Turkey's request for NATO support in protecting its border with Iraq. Neither variant flew combat missions during the war. However, the RF-104G did provide valuable reconnaissance information while patrolling the Turkey/Iraq border.

A lone Fiat G-222 transport was utilized to transport troops and equipment to and from Italy. It was supplemented by a C-130 Hercules of the 45th Aerobrigata. (Achille Vigna)

ARABIAN COALITION

Following the 2 August 1990 invasion of Kuwait, the only forces initially in place to halt any Iraqi thrust into Saudi Arabia, consisted of a loose coalition of Arabian countries. Although very well trained and equipped with state-of-the-art aircraft, the air arms of Saudi Arabia, Qatar, Bahrain and the United Arab Emirates stood little chance of stopping an all out Iraqi air and ground offensive.

Saudi Arabia fielded the largest air force in the region with more than two hundred modern aircraft. This force was further strengthened when the Royal Saudi Air Force took over administrative control of Kuwaiti Air Force aircraft which sought sanctuary in Saudi Arabia and Bahrain. When the air campaign began, the RSAF, and the Kuwaiti Air Force in exile, flew the bulk of offensive missions carried out by the Arabian Coalition. For the most part, its neighbors, Bahrain, Qatar and the UAE, flew local air defense missions in protection of their homeland.

Saudi Arabian Tornados flew a number of combat missions in conjunction with Tornados from the RAF and Italian Air Force. At the outset of the conflict, the RSAF possessed 36 Tornados, which were quite similar to the RAF GR.1. (British Aerospace)

On 24 January 1991, Capt. Al-Shamrani, from the RSAF, scored aerial victories against a pair of Exocet equipped Mirage F.1's. Both Mirages were downed by AIM-9 Sidewinders. A MiG-23 which was escorting the F.1's fled north. At the time of the engagement, Capt. Al-Shamrani was flying an F-15C, 80-068, from 42 Squadron, RSAF. (DOD)

The C-130 Hercules is utilized by countries around the world. The RSAF has utilized the type for several years as a transport and aerial refueling platform. (Brian C. Rogers)

The RSAF possesses a significant number of F-5Es. This example is a reconnaissance version assigned to 17 Squadron at Tabuk Saudi Arabia. (Keith Svendsen)

This RSAF KE-3A, from 18 squadron was based at Riyadh Saudi Arabia. Since the RSAF operates British and U.S. designed aircraft, its tanker fleet is equipped with flying boom and the hose and drogue aerial refueling system. (Andy Thomson)

Right and below: Qatar also utilized its force of Sea Kings and Gazelles during the conflict. (Peter Steinemann)

Below: On 2 August 1990, the RSAF had in its possession 24 Tornado F.3's from 29 and 34 squadrons. The type participated in CAP missions armed with Sky Flash and Sidewinder air-to-air missiles. (British Aerospace)

A number of Kuwaiti Air Force Skyhawks managed to find sanctuary in Saudi Arabia and Bahrain. Later brought under RSAF control at Dhahran, the type began flying combat operations on 17 January 1991. (DOD)

The Qatari Air Force also possessed a light attack capability with the Alpha Jet. It is not known whether any participated in the conflict. (Peter Steinemann)

Although small, the air arm of Bahrain nevertheless packs a potent punch with state-of-the-art aircraft such as this F-16D Falcon which flew defensive missions near its homeland. (General Dynamics)

IRAQI AIRCRAFT

This early version of the MiG-21 was mounted as a gate-guard at the entrance to Tallil Air Base which is situated southwest of the Iraqi town of Nasiriyah. Note the ever present portrait of Saddam Hussein. (J.P. Reilly)

Iraqi MiG-21 parked in the desert north of Tallil AB. Note the hastily applied camouflage which is nothing more than a mixture of sand and water. It must have been effective since this Iraqi fighter appears to have escaped damage. (J.P. Reilly)

An Air Force intelligence officer poses in the open cockpit of a MiG-21 at Tallil AB, Iraq. The aircraft was parked in the desert and covered with camouflaged netting. (J.P. Reilly)

A well worn and camouflaged MiG-27 found parked on a road within Tallil AB. This MiG may have escaped destruction because it was covered with tree limbs and a mixture of sand and water which was applied as another form of camouflage. (J.P. Reilly)

A basically intact Iraqi Hind helicopter at Tallil AB. The craft is equipped with a single air-to-ground rocket pod. (J.P. Reilly)

Another intact helicopter on the ramp at Tallil AB. This example, a Hip gunship, was shipped back to the states along with an Iraqi Hind also discovered at Tallil. Both are currently displayed at Ft. Rucker, Alabama. (J.P. Reilly)

OPERATION DESERT SHIELD/DESERT STORM PATCHES

DESERT STORM
NEVADA

GHOST RIDERS
416 TAC FTR SQDN

WE OWN THE NIGHT
OPERATION DESERT STORM

NIGHTSTALKERS
415 TAC FTR SQDN

38TH TAC RECON SQ

32
TAC FTR SQ (USAFE)

KANSAS COYOTES
117th AREFS

IRAQ BEACH PARTY
DESERT STORM
Sponsored by: KUWAITI KOOLER
ThanK You For Your Support

52ND TACTICAL FIGHTER WING

ATKRON 145

171st AIR REFUELING WING

81st TAC. FTR. SQ.

602D TACTICAL AIR CONTROL WG

174TH TACTICAL FIGHTER WING

344TH AREFS
CAPABLE – RELIABLE – VERSATILE

911TH AREFS
FIRST IN FLIGHT

READY WILLING ABLE
42D AIR REFUELING SQDN

DEATHANGELS
VMFA-235

POUR LA LIBERTE NOUS COMBATTONS
AIR WING TWO

HARM SHOOTER

ATKRON ONE FIVE FIVE

PROWLER

CARRIER AIR WING
3

SLUGGERS
FIGHTING 103

COMBAT CORSAIRS
IRAQ
BLUE HAWKS
ATTACK
NO SHELTER FROM THE STORM
ATTACK SQUADRON 72

BLUE HAWKS
ATKRON 72

DESERT STORM
91
COMBAT CRUISE

VAQ-130

DEUS Et PATRIA
FIGHTING-32

CARRIER AIR WING
FIVE

IRAQI INVITATIONAL
DESERT SHIELD
1990
1991
DESERT STORM
GULF TOURNAMENT

DESERT FOX
SADDAM DON'T SURF

DESERT STORM
TURKEY
SYRIA
IRAQ
ISRAEL
JORDAN
IRAN
SAUDI ARABIA
KUWAIT
PROWLER

AIR
8
WING

ROADRUNNERS
ATKRON 36

CVW
17

VS-32

VF1

DIAMONDBACKS

VF-102 DIAMONDBACKS

STARFIGHTERS
FIGHTING 33

FIGHTING 84

VAQ - 141

VMA-331

VMA-231

IN HOC SIGNO VINCES
VMA (AW) 533

VMFA 232

STARFIGHTER
F-104

XXX
TORNADO
F3

DESERT EAGLES
1990 1991
FIGHTING COCKS
43 (F) SQN

GLOSSARY

AAA Anti-Aircraft Artillery
AB Air Base
AFB Air Force Base
AFres Air Force Reserve
AGM Air-to-ground Missile
AIM Air Intercept Missile
ALARM Air-Launched Anti-Radar Missile
AMARC Aerospace Maintenance and Regeneration Center
ANG Air National Guard
ANGB Air National Guard Base
APC Armored Personnel Carrier
ASARS Advanced Synthetic Aperture Radar System
ASW Anti-Submarine Warfare
ASuW Anti-Surface Warfare
ATLIS Automatic Tracking Laser Illumination System
AWACS Airborne Warning And Control System
BAI Battlefield Air Interdiction
BarCAP Barrier Combat Air Patrol
B/N Bombardier/Navigator
BUFF Big Ugly Fat Fellow (B-52)
CAG Carrier Air Group
CAP Combat Air Patrol
CAS Close Air Support
CBU Cluster Bomb Unit
CV Aircraft Carrier (non nuclear)
CVN Aircraft Carrier (nuclear)
CVW Carrier Air Wing
DoD Department of Defense
ECM Electronic Counter Measures
ELINT Electronic Intelligence
EW Electronic Warfare
EWO Electronic Warfare Officer
FAC Forward Air Control
FLIR Forward-Looking Infra-Red
FOL Forward Operating Location
FRS Fleet Readiness Squadron
GBU Guided Bomb Unit
GPS Global Positioning System
HARM High-Speed Anti-Radiation Missile
HAVCAP High Asset Value Combat Air Patrol
IR Infrared
ISAR Inverse Synthetic Aperture Radar
J-STARS Joint Surveillance Target Attack Radar System
KTO Kuwait Theatre of Operations
LAMPS Light Airborne Multi-Purpose System
LANTIRN Low-Altitude, Navigation and Targeting, Infra-Red for Night
LGB Laser-Guided Bomb
LOROP LOng Range Oblique Photography
LST/CAM Laser Spot Tracker/Strike Camera
MAG Marine Air Group
MAW Military Airlift Wing or Marine Air Wing
MCAS Marine Corps Air Station
MEB Marine Expeditionary Brigade
MEF Marine Expeditionary Force
MER Multiple Ejector Rack
MiGCAP Combat Air Patrol to protect against enemy aircraft
MiG Sweep Mission to eliminate enemy air-to-air threat
NAS Naval Air Station
NFO Naval Flight Officer
Ordie Ordnanceman
PGM Precision Guided Munitions
RAF Royal Air Force
ResCAP Rescue Combat Air Patrol
RIO Radar Intercept Officer
RPV Remotely Piloted Vehicle
RSAF Royal Saudi Air Force
RNZAF Royal New Zealand Air Force
SAC Strategic Air Command
SAM Surface-to-Air Missile
SAR Search And Rescue
SEAD Suppression of Enemy Air Defenses
SLAM Standoff Land Attack Missile
SLAR Side-Looking Airborne Radar
SRW Strategic Reconnaissance Wing
SLUF Short Little Ugly Fellow (A-7)
Sortie A single mission flown by one aircraft
SuCAP Surface Combat Air Patrol
TAC Tactical Air Command
TALD Tactical Air-Launched Decoy
TARPS Tactical Air Reconnaissance Pod System
TFS Tactical Fighter Squadron
TFW Tactical Fighter Wing
TIALD Thermal Imaging And Laser Designator
TINS Thermal Imaging Navigation Set
TISEO Target Identification System Elector-Optical
TLAM Tomahawk Land-Attack Missile
TRAM Target Recognition and Attack Multisensor
TRS Tactical Reconnaissance Squadron
TRW Tactical Reconnaissance Wing
UAE United Arab Emirates
UAV Unmanned Air Vehicle
USAF United States Air Force
USAFE United States Air Force Europe
USMC United States Marine Corps
USN United States Navy
VA Navy Light Attack Squadron
VAQ Navy Electronic Warfare Squadron
VAW Navy Airborne Early Warning Squadron
VF Navy Fighter Squadron
VFA Navy Fighter and Attack Squadron
VMA Navy Medium Attack Squadron
VMA(AW) Marine Medium Attack Squadron (All Weather)
VMAQ Marine Electronic Warfare Squadron
VMFA Marine Fighter/Attack Squadron
VS Navy Anti-Submarine Squadron

Operation Desert Shield/Desert Storm
August 1990 – March 1991